SEX, DRUGS & ISLAM

AUTOBIOGRAPHY OF AN X FIGHTER PILOT

DARI GHAZNAVI

ISBN: 1484900766
ISBN 13: 9781484900765

This book is dedicated to my best friends, my children.

AUTHOR'S NOTE

One of the items on my bucket list was to tell my story, publish it for posterity, even make a difference. It's been a work in progress. Sometimes it may read like a diary written over many years. I have capitalized the first letter of any word that needed emphasis. This book is an honest, accurate and straightforward account of my life. Perhaps my story does contain some factual errors, for which I apologize. The memory, though rusty, is, for the most part, sufficiently intact.

I am compelled to share the lessons I learnt from challenging the sacred cows, and gaining the philosophical insights and observations about life, sex and religion. An epicurean approach to life is promoted along with the rejection and clear disdain of the religious fervor that plagues the Islamist world. Growing up in an Islamic culture, studying great religions and later choosing to live in the non-Muslim world, has given me a rather dispassionate, detached and fact-centered look at these religions and the hypocrisy of most of their followers. This autographical novel may read like an NC-17 version of "blow" and "top Gun," two movies that I love.

This juicy tell-all memoir will infuriate many true believers and be a disappointment to others. I have lived a remarkably unusual, dangerous and daring life, filled with action and packed with exciting flying and erotic adventures. Mine is the story of a controversial man living a unique life, rife with sexual escapades and serious brushes with the law.

Some readers will find my writing too offensive, graphic and violent. This book is not recommended for the young, faint-hearted or the easily offended. Among other things, this book recounts my involvement in illegal activities, including my experiences flying contraband merchandise, south of the border. This is also the heartbreaking narrative of a man who reinvented himself to attain redemption, which, some say, is the last refuge of a scoundrel.

I am thankful for my close friend and confidant, I. Rashid, whose help, covenant, encouragement and friendship sustained me through tough times.

Lastly, I am so eternally indebted to my Vigilant daughter, the great marvel of providential and somewhat human engineering. She pushed me hard to finish this project and went beyond the call of duty. Thank you, all from the core of my heart!

Dari
Winter 2014
Carlsbad, California.
darigi@gmail.com

TABLE OF CONTENTS   PAGE

FOREWORD

Almost half a century ago I climbed into a trainer cockpit with a young, ruggedly handsome lad aspiring to become an aviator. He would learn his craft well, turning out to be a very proficient and aggressive fighter pilot. Six years later; I would see the last of him as he emerged unscathed from a flaming fireball of an aircraft that had just crash-landed on the runway.

Fifty years later I would bump into a paraplegic on Facebook. I would recall the name and the face of that student of mine. We would connect once again. I would come to know of a life lived in a very different manner from mine. His had been a tumultuous and turbulent life; enviable, deplorable, commendable, lamentable all at once. As my mind reeled in amazement at how Ghaznavi had lived, I realized that it had one constant; excitement.

I am happy for my ex-student; equally, I am sad for him. I, however, have absolutely no desire to judge him. I do know one thing; I, the instructor, have, at this late stage in life, been taught a lot by this ex-student of mine. This book is a great instruction manual on how to live or how not to live.

The choice is yours.

Air Commodore (Retired) Shahid Khan
Dec '2013'

INTRODUCTION

In 2006, I was in my mid-fifties, a charming divorcé at the peak of a wonderful journey. I was dating a chick in her mid-twenties. Life was nonstop fun. I was dancing, body surfing and partying like a rock star on the Atlantic and Pacific coasts in the United States and South America.

I was making a ton of money, but I was getting sloppy, careless, even stupid. I flashed money, drove expensive cars in questionable neighborhoods, held wild parties at my beach pad and ran around with shady characters.

My pad was on a public street on Moonlight Beach, California. Public Beaches attract all kinds of people, including riffraff. I openly smoked pot and courted escorts. Women were in and out of my place so often that I should have had a revolving door.

My lifelong lucky streak was about to run out.

Arrogance, intolerance, and insolence were creeping in. Wasn't I the Master of the Universe? All good things must end? My bubble was about to burst, not with a pinprick, but with a fucking gunshot.

Around midnight on April Fool's Day, a man broke into my unlocked apartment while I was sleeping after a rather fantastic evening. Half asleep, I got up and confronted him. Although he was wearing a clown hat, glitter and make-up, I thought I recognized Devin, a shifty neighbor who had been at my place earlier that evening.

The intruder had a gun, I didn't see, and as I instinctively lunged at him, he fired at close range. The .22 bullet pierced my neck next to my Adam's apple and got lodged in the spinal column. Ouch, unfortunately, I survived, but the injury would paralyze me from the nipple line down. The incident put me in a wheelchair for life.

At the time, I was certain that I knew my attacker. However, now I am not 100 percent sure that it was my neighbor. Then who? I didn't have any enemies that I knew of who would want me dead.

An investigation followed. The detective said he recommended that the District Attorney (D.A.) issue a warrant for Devin's arrest. Six months after the shooting, I got a call from the D.A. that shocked me. I almost fell out of my wheelchair.

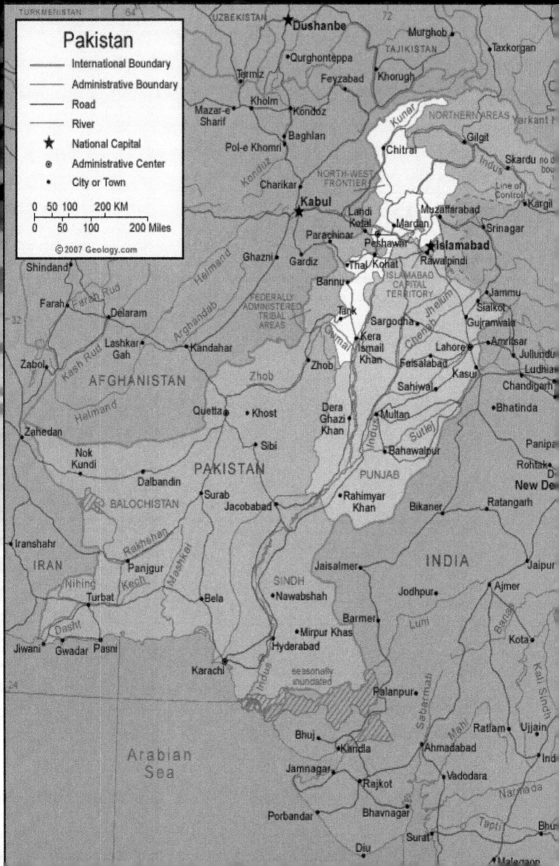

1

BACKGROUND

I was born in Pakistan, which was once part of India, and before that, it was the home of many ancient empires, including that of my ancestors, the Ghaznavid Dynasty.

India, for two centuries, was the 'Jewel' **colony in** the British crown. In 1947, the British reluctantly relinquished control of India, yielding to the nonviolent protests of Mahatma Gandhi, Mohammad Ali Jinnah, and others. The Partition, as it is called, plunged India into communal genocide and mayhem.

Chaos erupted, resulting in the deaths of (reportedly) a staggering two Million innocent people and the displacement of millions more. Muslim and Hindu neighbors turned on each other overnight. Mob frenzy prevailed; the cruelty was unimaginable. Murderous gangs from both religions committed horrific crimes, participating in gang rapes, burning neighborhoods and carrying out ethnic cleansing.

Two countries were created based on religion, a giant geopolitical blunder in my opinion. Hindu populated areas were named

India, and areas of Muslim majority were called Pakistan—the land of the pure—which it is anything but.

This very deeply and deadly religious Islamic country, corrupted to its core, is strategically located near the mouth of the Straits of Hormuz in the Arabian Sea, through which roughly 35 percent of oil tankers pass, headed for the Western nations. Potential disruption of the safe passage of oil traffic poses an ongoing threat to the United States and her allies.

Whereas secular India would flourish as a democracy, Muslim Pakistan would falter and stay mired, decaying for decades under military rule.

Pakistan is a rogue and marginally failed state, perpetually rocked by political instability and military rule. The country has always been an explosive sectarian, tribal and religious powder keg looking for a fuse to ignite. It has a serious terrorism problem, which America unintentionally triggered with its war on terror, resulting in Pakistan becoming collateral damage. Now the country is coming apart at the seams. Drone attacks, while successful in their mission, have pissed off the locals.

To top it off, Pakistan, with its India-centric policies, has acquired over one hundred nuclear weapons and F-16s, thanks to the United States of America, her fair-weather friend.

My motherland started a super-secret nuclear program in the 1970s under the controversial and contentious rule of the brilliant and mercurial Prime Minister Z.A. Bhutto. A legendary ultranationalist leader, Mr. Bhutto was executed in 1979, framed by his handpicked Chief of Army Staff (and later president of Pakistan) Muhammad Zia-ul-Haq.

Ironically Zia was killed in a mysterious and fiery Hercules C-130 airplane crash in 1988. The VVIP plane, Pak One, took off ahead of a storm and rose up in clear skies, but after two minutes and thirty seconds, the Bahawalpur tower lost radio contact with the plane. The C-130 flew low and then plunged from the sky and hit the ground with such furious force that it was blown to pieces, its wreckage scattered over a large area. Among the thirty-one dead were the top generals of Pakistan along with, American ambassador, Arnold Raphel, and his military attaché, General Herbert Wassom.

Curiously, the pilot of Pak One was my old badge mate from our academy years, a rather unremarkable fellow by the name of Wing Commander Mashood Hassan. He had previously confided in an associate, saying that he hated President Zia and held him responsible for the murder of a local religious figure, that Mashood fancied. He reportedly remarked, "The day Zia flies with me that will be his last flight." By the way, it was also Mashood's last day on earth. Go figure!

The fanatically religious General ruled Pakistan with draconian laws and transformed a moderate country into an Islamist State. He hoodwinked President Reagan for years into getting Pakistan billions in arms. The General's rule gave birth to hundreds of Madrases—Islamist seminaries—thus producing legions of future Jihadis, with their rigid medieval ideology rooted in Sharia laws. Jihadi is a self-described religious warrior who is willing to give up their life in the name of Islam, a terrible misguided chivalry.

They mistakenly think crusaders are here all over again, led by America.

Faithful Islamists churn out suicide bombers in droves, even sacrificing their own children like lambs as Prophet Abraham once intended to do centuries ago. Because life lacks pleasure, death has no terror. These militant Islamists may have the courage of their conviction, what they lack is the wisdom to get their righteous heads out of their asses.

Listen, the American military is stronger and more lethal than the next seven military powers combined. How is that for statistical madness? You don't fuck with Uncle Sam. But nobody is listening. Faith has screwed up generations of Muslims, led by Pakistan and Iran.

Nations are made up of people. A country, like a human being, has to earn its respect. Blind loyalty and uncritical respect for one's country of birth is misguided. Countries, like people, must be held to the highest standards of conduct, station, and achievement. The admiration or rebuke ought to be hard earned and/or well deserved.

Whereas America has my hard-earned respect, my native Pakistan does not deserve it. I can not respect a country that shamefully has only 2 percent of the world's population, but has more militants than the rest of the world put together.

After sheltering Osama bin Laden in a garrison city for years, Pakistan has unwisely hid the top leadership of the Taliban including Mullah Omar, the reclusive one-eyed supremo. No one knows where the supremo is?

O' please, Pakistan, who are you kidding?

2

CHILDHOOD

T HE exact date of my birth is unknown as accurate and cred-
ible birth records were not kept in parts of Pakistan then.
Approximation and triangulation put it around the time of
the assassination of the country's first Prime Minister, Liaqat
Ali Khan, which occurred on 16 October 1951. So pick a date
around his death, like I did when I became a naturalized citizen
of the United States of America. That was one of the happiest
days of my life, second only to my graduation in 1972, as a pilot
officer in the elite Pakistan Air Force.

This fantastic, charmed and somewhat bittersweet journey
starts in Hyderabad, Sindh.

I was delivered by a midwife without my consent, my parents
named me, Iqtidar Mustafa Ghaznavi, that I detested. This geographical accident placed me in the epicenter of a harsh, backward and poor country. Sixth child of our family of eleven, I
grew up as the black sheep in a middle-class, chaotic household,
living in this ghetto, awful, Sin city.

The ancestral land of Sindh has a rich and colorful history, where descendants of the Arab travelers, conquerors, and truth seekers would converge, battle and settle. They were known to be lovers of truth, wisdom and knowledge. Due to their saintliness, devotion, and wisdom, they were revered as 'Peer Saeen.'

Hyderabad is located in the ancient Indus Valley. Growing up, I felt as if I was in the asshole of the universe. Too many people were crammed into this crowded, loud and unbearable place.

Malarial mosquitoes, fecal flies, fire ants and numerous other ungodly insects competed with each other to get a piece of your brown ass. Pedestrians ran into each other in streets that were jammed with rickshaws, cars, camels, cows, donkey carts and any other form of transportation. Hordes of beggars and juvenile gangs roamed the city in search of food, money, equality, revenge and you name it. Hot winds blew in from the eastern, oven-like deserts of Rajistan, India, making this a very unforgiving and brutal environment. Time seemed to stand still in this tinderbox, forgotten by the rest of the world.

Very little is known or documented about my father's family or my grandfather. It was all hush-hush, and we never saw or knew much about them. My father, Maulana Fazl Ahmed Ghaznavi, was an Afghan migrant who settled in Sindh, around the first part of the twentieth century.

My paternal grandfather, Sardar Allah Bux Ghaznavi, was a senior officer in the Afghan army. Grandpa was rumored to have been executed in Kabul in the late 1920s due to his part in a failed mutiny during the rule of King Amanullah Khan of the God granted kingdom of Afghanistan. Because of his alleged treason, my father's remaining family members fled to neighboring Quetta, Baluchistan.

On 31 May 1935, at 3:02 a.m., a deadly earthquake hit Quetta, killing approximately fifty-thousand people, including all my paternal family members except my father, who was doing Islamic missionary work, hundreds of miles away in Sindh, then part of British India.

My father, we called him Abaji, was a master chess player and taught me this game. We played chess almost every night. He would often win, till later when I started winning. The game of chess teaches one, the Machiavellian tricks like; to be shrewd, to plan ahead and anticipate the opponent's moves and take pre-emptive action.

On my last trip to Hyderabad before his death in the late eighties, we had a vigorous conversation about his family, our religion, and our culture. I challenged him on his Islamic beliefs, which I strongly disagreed with. He was somewhat disturbed by my logical arguments. While he stuck to faithful lines, I followed the logic of the issuesThe student was checkmating the teacher. Before I left to go home to Alaska, he confided in me and whispered, "Son, I thought I was going to heaven for sure, but after talking to you, I am not so sure. You have put doubts in my mind, and now I am uncertain where I'm going after I die." He laughed.

I was sad to hear that, I should have let him pass in peace. Is ignorance a bliss? Should one refrain from speaking one's truth, if it is going to hurt or perturb another? My Sufi father was a kind and liberal whirling dervish. After losing his entire family in the Quetta earthquake, dad never returned to Afghanistan. He became an Arabic teacher in the local high school attended by us five brothers.

In my early teens, I woke up at dawn to see my bearded father sitting cross-legged, Buddha-like pose in the front yard. He would be gently reciting verses of the Quran in a loud, though melodious voice, perhaps to wake us children up. We slept outside in the veranda where the hot days gave way to the cool desert breezes blowing under starry nights and clear skies.

Each morning, my portly mother would milk her two cows and then pour a glass of raw milk for each of her sons—not daughters—saying, "Rise and shine son, it's time for morning prayers." An old woman's tale mistakenly claimed that the milk should be drunk straight out of a cow's saggy tits.

My dutiful mother then made dad breakfast that included four eggs, white toast, and marmalade jam. After breakfast, Abaji read several newspapers that were hand-delivered daily to our house. The newspapers were written in three local languages.

As a preschooler, I would accompany dad to the main market in a rickshaw. We bought fresh vegetables, many kinds of fruits and just-cut red meat dripping with blood. We also bought many other items, including exotic items such as goat brains and balls, which were foolishly thought to be good for strength. He frequently bought a live chicken for lunch. The frightened chicken was later slaughtered by him or the servant in a kosher manner called 'Halal.' Muslims are mandated to consume Halal meat only. I would practice this novel form of chicken execution that hardened me to blood and gore, along with physiology and biology lessons. Pork is forbidden in Islam. Pigs are considered filthy, shot on sight.

Abaji made an effort to educate us on political, religious, historical and international affairs. Like me, he was a political junkie immersed in books, magazines and newspapers, generally seen reading or writing. He had only a few friends, and they too drifted away as we grew older. His books and his children were his world. We had no Tv, only a crappy radio.

He hoped that one of us five boys would join the military, rise to power and inspire a revolution. He dreamed of uniting the countries of India, Pakistan and Afghanistan into a single empire named 'Islamistan.'

Mom was an innocent, loving and unread homemaker, a Punjabi from an extremely humble background. Dad's disregard for mother's family plus his philandering strained their relationship. In this testosterone-fueled male chauvinistic society, women are often relegated to the back benches of the hierarchy. Mom was no exception. Mother was unaware of the world beyond Islam, jewelry, housekeeping and motherhood. Discipline and punishment were her forte.

Once an Imam of the local mosque, my dad's luck would change and so would his life, for the worse. He temporarily became wealthy. Was it Lord Acton who said, "Power corrupts and absolute power corrupts absolutely." Well, it surely did.

The well-off and affluent were well known in 'Chukla', the notorious red light district. Chukla was a dark, dingy and sleazy area in the center of Hyderabad where partiers partook in whiskey, dance, sex and gambling. At night, music filtered out of the windows of the dilapidated buildings. Child prostitutes were raised with an eye toward their potential high value. Virgin girls were in high demand and commanded premium prices in this land of the pure.

Prostitution is common and somewhat legal in the Islamic world. It is common knowledge that most of these holy men live double lives. While they preach piety and purity from their pulpits, behind the scenes their extramarital sexual and homosexual activities are well known and ridiculed countrywide.

Some of my scary, strange and slimy memories of childhood and puberty belong in Chukla where girls, dancing, and booze drew me early to this erotic zone. At age eleven or twelve, I would sneak out of our house after dark and go to this notorious district. The high and mighty of Sindh were often seen, slowly cruising the narrow, pot- holed streets in their Pajero jeeps and other fancy vehicles. Their conspicuous armed guards sat menacingly in the open-air back seats. The system turned a blind eye to this dark underbelly and liberal interpretation of Islam. Contradictions exist in nature too.

I learned early to wish loved one's health, happiness, and peace, but not too much wealth. Fame and fortune corrode the human spirit and pollute the soul. I saw it up front. Dad shrewdly married our eldest sister to this fabulously rich and famous man. His son-in-law, the 'Peer of Hala' would make him rich temporarily, as dad was to squander the newly found wealth on the usual sins of the flesh; Sex and booze, within a few years.

Look at the lottery winners in the United States, most of them are ruined by their money within a couple of years of winning their jackpots. Notice how young men and women who earn ungodly sums of money in the sports and entertainment world, go berserk with their earnings, making fools of themselves. Thoughtful people would agree that not too much money should be left to one's undeserving children as an inheritance will often spawn a fight among siblings. With excess money, all kinds of avenues and options open up. The Devil goes to work, and temptations are almost impossible to overcome. I do not wish too much wealth on anyone, even myself.

The obnoxious behavior of the rich and mighty repulsed me. It made me a bit impervious to the temptations of power, fame and wealth. (However, I could not master the passions of the flesh.)

Possessions, hoarding, and materialism turned me off early and money making for the sake of making money was never my principle in life. I worked hard and let the chips fall where they may, and let the results be my guide. At the end of the day, I was happy with the outcome of my efforts, accepting what I was capable of producing at that moment, no more, no less. Furthermore, I swore not to live under a tyrannical system when I got older and became independent. I was a rebel with a strong desire to get the hell out of Pakistan. Wouldn't You feel that way?

I am not materialistic, generally quite simple. When divorced from my Ex in 2001, I moved out with all my belongings fitting snugly into my Lexus. I am wired from my iPhone to my MacBook and iPad. I am on my laptop right now, writing this book with just one functioning middle finger, the one with which you flip the bird. Rest of the fingers do not work.

To me, sheep-like adherence to religious doctrines was simply unacceptable. I chose not to follow the herd. I felt I was surrounded by imbeciles, thereby developing a major disconnect with locals. However, I did notice the good that faith was doing for many ordinary, simple folks, like my mother, six sisters, and countless others whose lives were being greatly enriched by their faith. The power of prayer and faith is quite evident in all cultures

I tried to learn, to listen, remain calm and not talk as much, as I was by nature a braggadocio, a blabbermouth. Say what comes to mind, regret it later. I'd remind myself that knowledge is gained with the ears and not the tongue, the strongest muscle in the body. Maybe that is why nature designed us to have a single tongue and two ears.

3

ADOLESCENT YEARS

HAVING no faith in traditional gods or established beliefs, I lived by my own codes. I felt endowed with extra-ordinary powers of deep reflection and objective thinking. Rene Descartes's phrase "I think, therefore, I am" elevated me to a unique spirituality. I felt blessed despite my rejection of religions or the existence of a God, many gods or no God.

Mine was mostly an Agnostic approach; I was quite certain that I had no way to ascertain such weighty issues. No one does, and those who say they do, despite their sincerity, are simply blowing through their butt holes. Most people feel defeated and give in to Faith and take the easy way out, not thinking too hard for themselves. Plus our vacant mind slates have been written on, by our upbringing. We equate respect for elders with validity of their faith. I was unconcerned about the meaning or the purpose of, or the end of life. Importantly, if a cause and effect pay off, I regard it as my personal triumph, not a celestial reward.

At times though, I wish I were a believer as it makes things easier. Go along, get along. Don't create waves and rock the boat. Alas, I am not built that way. I am the ultimate skeptic, questioning and scrutinizing everything and everyone—the Socratic approach. I remind myself that Socrates was forced to drink poison (hemlock) for allegedly corrupting the youth with his teachings.

I am told that I am an intellectual flame thrower, challenging and questioning centuries' old sacred beliefs, sacred cows, dogmas and cultural practices, turning them on their heads, I never could express myself while living in a Muslim culture. My book will be banned, banished from the bookshelves.

Does God exist? Does life have a purpose? Why were we born, and where are we going after death? How in the hell would anyone know about such abstract concepts? No one has been to hell and back. Have you?

I was quite content to know what I knew and accept what I did not know. Only God would know. That old serenity prayer ought to be inscribed on all those who aspire to excel.

God grant me the serenity to accept the things I cannot change, the Courage to change the things I can, and the wisdom to know the difference.

Beautiful. I didn't want to accept at face value what men and books supposedly said centuries ago, when men were cruel and science was in its infancy. We are so foolish; bad brains everywhere. We can't even agree on simple matters. Take a day off and cruise down to your local courthouse. The courts are packed with warring parties fighting, disagreeing on matters that confound court personnel and spectators alike. Ask any lawyer what inane bull, he or she goes through every day.

A mind that makes one believe nonsense that great religions purport would also lead one to arrive at erroneous assumptions and faulty conclusions on other important matters of life. Can you imagine a court of law based on faith alone?

Albert Einstein, a freethinker, succinctly put it in similar words, saying that the religion a man or woman believes in is that of the community in which he or she lives. It is the influence of the environment that determines the faith in question. Einstein further states, "I believe in Spinoza's God who reveals himself in the orderly harmony of what exists, not in a God who concerns himself with the fates and actions of human beings."

Due to my outrageous behavior as a kid, I was regularly given severe whippings by my elders. People would hound my parents because I had beaten up their son, eyed their daughter or run out on a restaurant bill.

Any advance on a female was considered molestation, mutual or not. Being a Romeo, I was always on the prowl for chicks to have innocent, clandestine affairs as formal dating was not allowed. The regressive culture frowned on male-female relationships, which made the forbidden fruit all the sweeter.

In early teens, I had an affair with another teenager, who lived across the street. I had a routine of studying late into the night. Around midnight, I would sneak out of my room and go over to her house. She would come to meet me by her living room window with iron bars. On a cold night, we were making out in the dark when the lights came on, and I saw her shocked father standing over us with a rifle leveled at me.

He was beside himself to see his daughter in a boy's arms. She scurried out of the room. Her angry father pointed the barrel of his antique rifle at my face, pointed toward the gate and gestured me to get the fuck off the premises. Scared shitless, I retreated slowly, thinking that the bastard was going to shoot me in the ass. That was the end of my short and sweet affair with Moni.

The 1958 movie *Horror of Dracula* scared the living shit out of me. I am sure you would be just as shit scared watching Dracula alone at age seven or eight. I would Not go out in the dark for a long, long time. Dracula was real; he was coming after me. He was only waiting for the sun to set.

Later when I moved to the West, I would go out to discotheques to dance regularly. Dancing has always been my passion and girls, my obsession. While young and strong in the late 1970s, I would throw myself in the mosh pits at clubs, dancing and brawling to punk rock bands until, one night at the Hollywood Bowl, a young marine made me cry uncle. I love music. Who doesn't? Even the dull and boring do. Music makes one happy, makes you want to dance, changes mood and alters brain chemistry, totally. When dancing, I noticed that one is a happy camper. Look around, you hardly ever see scowling faces on the dance floor.

Being a hopeless romantic, a tortured Romeo, I love to love, be in love and be loved by a woman, not Bill or Bob. Despite rumors to the contrary, I don't swing both ways and have no identity issues. Although to the dismay of some of my family and friends, I occasionally like to wear Lipstick and Earrings. I used to go to gay and lesbian dance clubs often; I think those clubs are fun. Strange fascination!

I think gays, lesbians, bisexuals, transsexuals and other cross dressers are great. It's all beautiful as each has a proper and natural place, without which the human tapestry would be incomplete.

Here is an interesting phenomenon: Cultures put a premium on skin color. Fair or light skin is prized and preferred worldwide. The fairer the color, the higher the demand in the marketplace. Where I come from, every mother looks for a light-skinned daughter-in-law. Black is not considered beautiful.

In younger days, I wanted to look fairer than my tan skin. Yes, I was insecure about my looks. I would not go out in the sun much; I even would run from shade to shade. I used to apply powder on my face to appear fairer, like Michael Jackson did. Before I met someone who I thought liked me, I would put on light makeup to look pretty, like chicks do. I carried powder on me. Brainwashed? I passed this gene on to my younger daughter.

When she was two or three, Geena wanted to be a white girl. She called herself Amy, the name of her babysitter, who sat on my face quite often. Ouch, that hurt.

When you go to the mosque, church, synagogue or other house of worship, are you there to please your God? I disagree. May I suggest that you are there for number one, you, and rightly so. You are primarily there, begging for peace, money, health and whatever else, always asking for something. You think your (imaginary) God cares about your prayers? Even if God exists, why would He care about You, who may have just arrived there after screwing your neighbor's spouse? Not that you have—you wish. You are there because you want Something, or worse, you might be dutifully, mindlessly, practicing the religion of your parents and their parents. Ever think about that?

What if you were born into my family. Chances are close to zero that you would become, anything but Muslim. Do you think I would have been Muslim, had I been born as your brother in your every Wednesday and Sunday born-again family? No, my brother and sister, no. A Snake from a snake and corn from corn. One doesn't plant cauliflower and get bananas. You are who you are because you were born in that household, in that community, in that country. It's quite simple, really.

The first job I ever had, I was around eleven, working as a cashier, conductor, on the public buses my father owned, a mini Greyhound. Constantly counting money helped my mathematical skills, which are essential, even critical, for success in business. The bus would leave before sunrise and return after dark. We traveled all day to different destinations hundreds of miles away, picking up or dropping off passengers in antique, fucked up buses with mechanic onboard.

Whenever we saw someone flagging us down, we stopped and picked up the ride, even if we were packed full. Passengers were crammed one on top of each other. Every passenger was money in the bank. I loved hanging out by the door, escaping the stench of the riders and feeling the wind on my face while the bus traveled at high speeds. It was like riding a motorcycle.

I was precocious, sharp and street smart. I was also shrewd, cunning and calculating, always looking out for number one, Me. I always had pockets full of rupees, as I would steal my dad blind. Stealing, fencing, slinging, lying and sneaking around became my everyday routine. I was quick and crooked. I started developing bad habits at an early age. Bad habits are like a comfortable bed; they are easy to get into, but hard to get out of.

Wheeling and dealing came natural to me and serves me well to this day. Deal making was to become my passion in life. At the end of the day, I am not a happy camper if I haven't made a deal, any deal, preferably an airplane deal, but, I would settle for some strange sex ... Smiles. Most of us would or should, except the prude, the dead and the sincerely in love. Making money is only the byproduct of deal making. Thankfully, I like making, but not spending it, and when you don't spend it, money starts to pile up. Can you relate?

I developed an affinity with the West early and started following news of the English speaking countries and learning Western ways. The Mother East bored me to tears. I paid special attention to learning English and carried a pocket dictionary that translated English into Urdu, Sindhi, and Punjabi. Now I speak all four languages fluently. I would have geographical, political and spelling competitions with friends. We spoke Punjabi at home, attended a Sindhi-speaking school and most of my friends spoke Urdu. All the schools I attended were segregated, rough. I never went to coed schools. Perhaps that's one reason my life has been a twisted tale of lust, alienation and angst about women.

We were not rich; only pretended to be, which angered me, and I often fought with my family because of it. Our relation to my super rich brother-in-law, Baba Saeen, had its downside.

We were wannabe rich. Money came and went, only the pretense remained.

Nobody paid much attention to a young, dark, innocent looking boy. Looks can be deceptive. To get noticed, I made scenes and acted stupidly. I made my parents worried sick by staying out late at night. As President Theodore Roosevelt—I walked softly but carried a big dick, I meant stick, Smiles. I swore not to instill such false values in my would-be children. They would be thankful when they grew up.

I dreamed of living in America and having a white girl as a girlfriend. The very thought of that would make me cream my pants. It seemed within my grasp. I hated my loser life in Pakistan. Help, get me out of here.

In my Gangsta world, street fighting was both a passion and a necessity. We were lawless hooligan gang bangers, but we did not drink or do drugs. They just weren't part and parcel of our growing up. Only the low-life, the scum, got high, mostly on hashish or heroin. The rich drank heavily but drank only Scotch, generally making fools of themselves. I never drank until I moved to the West.

I have always been fascinated by the underbelly of society. Crime and violence thrilled me. I was messed up. Lacking adult guidance, I had no respect for most elders or authority and no moral or religious compunctions. Soon the verbal arguments and fist fights turned into knives and guns, giving me a pause as I was a pretty boy afraid of getting facial scars. I already had several of them, making me unhappy.

In this strict Islamic, segregated and somewhat homosexual culture, I fought off several molestations and rape attempts. I grew up with six sisters, using their makeup to look pretty, thereby attracting lecherous men to me. Lacking female contact, men would routinely but secretly prey on pretty boys. Incest was more common than was acknowledged.

One time, when I was about twelve, I had a frightening experience. We were visiting a distant uncle who lived hundreds of miles away in a small town called Jamesabad. We had traveled there by train, the most common way of travel in Pakistan. The British did leave a few good things behind; the railroad system stands out. An adult friend of our hosts offered to take me swimming in a river couple of miles away. I learned to swim in rivers. I was crazy about rapid river currents, so I jumped at the chance offered by this adult. We walked to get to the river.

Once we reached a thick jungle by the river, he suddenly, right out of the blue, grabbed me by the neck, took out a long switch-blade knife and held it against my throat, telling me to drop my pants or else. Terror struck. If rape is inevitable, should one lay back, even enjoy it or fight back and risk injury or death? I had only seconds to decide. Trickery? To disarm him, I pretended I was a fellow traveler. I did some fine acting, touching his genitals and assuring him that I, too, was into it, a fellow faggot.

The son of a bitch fell for the trick, smiled fiendishly and put the knife away. He relaxed, started undressing and stroking himself. As he turned and kneeled on the riverbank to get a drink, I pushed him as hard as I could. He fell over the bank into the raging river and was swept down by the current. Horrified, I ran as fast as I could. He came running after me, cursing, half naked, with his shalwar pants in one hand and the knife in the other. I was a fast runner and the sport came in handy. I barely made it safely to my relatives' house and blurted about the incident.

Word of the attempted rape spread quickly. The next thing I knew, all the enraged elders of the village got together, marched to the child molester's shack, dragged him out of his mud house and beat the crap out of him. I was in the forefront, kicking his ass encouraged by onlookers. Seeing him bloody from our beatings and squealing like a pig left me satisfied. Street justice was served. Revenge and retribution were sweet. Later in life, I would learn the futility of these evil twins. For now, I learned how to deal with would-be attackers, if faced with any future episodes. And there were a couple more.

I had an ugly childhood. I was a royal pain in the ass to my parents. They put me in a boarding school for boys for two years, hoping for my redemption. By my early teens, I had become an expert thief, liar, and a cheat, dabbling in illegal, nefarious and shabby activities. I was a slimy, small time Crook, avoided by many. The boarding school was unable to tame me. I frequently climbed the school wall and disappeared into the crowded streets. I was up to no good. I ran away any chance I got. The boarding school finally got tired of my shenanigans and expelled me.

I always felt that I was not an ordinary boy, not like anyone else. I thought of myself as special, destined to do great things, if only I could stay alive and out of jail. I ran away from home, traveling hundreds of miles to my aunt's house in Lahore so that I could go to a better school and get a fresh start. Lacking transportation and wearing ill-fitting shoes and tight teddy pants, I walked miles and miles in the scorching heat from one institution to another, but in vain. Riding in a bus was not my thing as buses were full of foul smelling people. Deodorant was a novelty used in the West.

I couldn't get admission. Grades mattered, but influence and nepotism ruled. I kept trying, hoping that one of the schools would accept me. Aristotle once said, "Hope is a walking dream" the last thing to die.

Disappointed, I returned to Hyderabad, only to be treated with disdain and indifference by the family. Mother, the disciplinarian, had ordered everyone to give me the cold shoulder when I returned, sort of an unwelcome back home. I was miserable. I thought I wanted to be an engineer because it was what everyone else wanted to be.

Education was important to me. I recognized it as a prerequisite for and a gateway to success. A one-way ticket to the West?

4

PAKISTAN AIR FORCE

B EING a metrosexual boy, I was afraid to get physically hurt as
I hung out with a rough crowd. Gang fights were common.
On a regular basis, we bloodied each other. I was a lean, mean
fighting machine, feared or respected by most other local mini
wannabe gangsters. The police did not scare me, nor did they
ordinarily intervene in the hood.

People settled their scores among themselves. The police were
corrupt and looked the other way unless the crime was serious.
Street justice prevailed. It was the law of the jungle, functional
in a dysfunctional way. You made peace with your circumstances.
Human beings are malleable, adaptable to any condition, even
if incarcerated in Siberia.

I was getting tired and somewhat scared of the environment
and circumstances I found myself in. Chickens were coming
home to roost. I felt the looming danger of getting knifed, shot
or seriously hurt. I thought I should go away before I regretted
it, so I decided to go legit, take fighting to another level, join the
ultimate fighting machine, the Military.

Pakistan Air Force is highly competitive and accepted only the nation's crème de la crème. Even getting Selected to be a pilot was huge, let alone graduating from the academy. Air Force officers are well respected and envied. As the pilot of a fighter jet, I thought I could legally and proudly fight and inflict maximum damage on India or on any other country, like our neighbors, Iran and Afghanistan, with whom we had simmering hostilities and an uneasy truce.

My eldest sister was married to this noble, respectable and dignified Sindhi tycoon. He was a legendary Sufi poet, *Peer of Hala,* the spiritual leader of millions. His dynasty and Raj was dated centuries back. People would lower their eyes and bow out of respect when his motorcade passed. We affectionately called him 'Baba Saeen.' He was a man of enormous wealth and political influence. Baba Saeen was one of the very few people in my shitty life who had my respect and admiration.

My brother-in-law was an icon of civility, nobility and simplicity and one of the nicest and worthiest men I have known. He was a tall, well mustached, handsome man with a grand and towering personality that inspired and motivated the masses. My dignified man had inherited the crown of his centuries-old dynasty. He owned hundreds of indentured servants. Yes, Feudalism is still alive and well in many parts of the underdeveloped world.

In the summer of 1970, I was on a break from the Air Force Academy, which I had joined earlier in 1968. Our family members were vacationing at Baba Saeen's vast estate in Hala, a rural town thirty miles from Hyderabad. I had both a thrilling, but a tragic, thing happen.

Hala is a primitive place that has a very special place in my heart. I carry extremely fond memories of growing up in Hala. We spent our vacations at Baba Saeen's majestically sprawling estate. Because of him, we were treated like royalty. I grew up playing with his many sons, my fabulously rich, powerful and famous nephews. They are my good friends who live royal and princely lives in Pakistan. They are involved in the higher echelons of the government, influencing local and national politics and commanding respect and gratitude from millions, including me.

Baba Saeen owned dozens of well-bred Arabian and quarter horses. He had a personal stallion, a brown mustang. Because of his health, Baba Saeen had stopped riding the horse. The caretaker of the stable kept the stallion well fed and groomed, but the horse never got any exercise as no one was allowed to, or dared to, ride the master's personal horse. Horses like to run, but this baby wasn't running; he was just being richly fed and getting lazy, fat.

One day, I must have been bored, restless or seeking action. It was a balmy summer day with temperatures hovering around 120 degrees Fahrenheit. Horseback riding was one of my passions. Baba Saeen had a stable full of horses, but I had my eye on his personal horse. I wanted to take his prized possession for a spin. I approached him, "Baba Saeen, could I be granted the permission to ride your horse, sir?" Baba Saeen looked slightly Puzzled at this daring request. Perhaps it was the only time he ever had such a request from anyone. Baba Saeen hesitated but before he could say no, I quickly offered to show him my military credentials. I assured him of my strength, stamina, and training. I told him that I was a capable rider and that I was on the Air Force polo team, a slight exaggeration. The Air Force had no polo team, but I badly wanted to ride the horse.

Baba Saeen relented but cautioned me to be careful as that big beauty had not been ridden for years. I was ecstatic and honored that I would be trusted to ride the horse. He politely ordered me to obtain the consent of my equally dignified sister, cautioning me that it could be a dicey ride. I was bursting out of my skin to run to the stable. I politely shrugged my shoulders. Who thinks about safety at a young age? One feels immortal and invincible as a young adult, especially a street smart, battle-hardened bad boy like me. You think you will stay young and live forever.

Once given the royal permission, I run to the stable a quarter mile away. I relayed Baba Saeen's order to the shocked stable keeper and told him to saddle up. Even the horse looked pleasantly shocked. Once ready, I took the reins from the bewildered keeper and voilà! The world was my oyster.

I galloped the horse at lightning speeds for hours along the mighty Indus river. We must have been a sight to behold with the horse's mane flowing in the air and me sitting ramrod straight in the saddle. As usual, the hot desert wind was blowing under the scorching midday sun. I didn't notice or care. The horse seemed very happy and made short, but high pitched *EEE* sounds out of excitement. The sounds must have echoed throughout the village. The happy horse and I got along great and had a wild time together.

Exhausted and sweating profusely, we returned to the stable. I kissed the neck of this beautiful perspiring horse. With his tail held high, he pawed the ground with his front foot. I patted him on his neck a few times, thanked him and gave the reins to the happy and wide-eyed stable keeper. I left to go brag about my magnificent magic carpet ride to anyone who would listen.

My puffed up pride would be short lived.

The word had spread like wildfire, and HaIa was wonder-struck to see the master's horse had been ridden by this proud and pugnacious young man. The few hones in Hala started to buzz, informing the palace that I was loose galloping master's horse.

The palace people were impressed, and I was beaming like a peacock with superiority and conceit. An hour later, to our shock and horror, calamity struck; the poor horse collapsed and died. Heat stroke? We had failed to walk the stud around to cool him off before putting him out to pasture. A horrible mistake. Holy shit.

The village was grief stricken, even mad at me. To my surprise, Baba Saeen was gracious and stoic about his loss. He even congratulated me for being a good rider. There he was, a true prince, an aristocrat of giant proportion. He was such an incredible ideal of a man. They don't make people like him anymore. The incident taught me to deal with reality, poignantly and accept the way of the nature, the way the cookie crumbles. My shit stinks just like yours.

I am remembered in Hala as Baba Saeen's horse killer.

In 1967, I had quit Jamshoro Engineering college, where I was a freshman. I applied to join the Air Force as a fighter pilot. I read that America would be landing a man on the moon shortly, which the clergy refused to believe. Complete denial.

After a rigorous competitive selection process that included a flight aptitude test and thorough psychological and medical examinations, I was selected.

I was admitted to the Pakistan Air Force academy as a flight cadet for a three years pilot course, called 52nd GDP. I had never known such joy. A game changer? I was the envy of my peers. People put a premium value on PAF pilots. They are the most respected group in the Armed forces, in the entire nation. And to boot, Chicks dug pilots. "Sorry sweetie, I am late."

The PAF Academy is located near Murree, a hill station about 8,000 feet above the capital, Islamabad, on the southern slopes of the Himalayas. It is an institution that most young men would kill to be in. The summer capital of the British Raj with its Neo-Gothic architecture and snowy winters and pleasant summers.

The military system is designed to give you a colossal shock—a major jolt—when you arrive. A little attitude re-adjustment—forcibly rearranging the furniture of your mind.

It's the end of life as you know it. For a starter, they shave your head on arrival. Getting new identity? My cherished, long curly hair was shaved off by a giggling, but servile, barber. And that is not funny, ok, I told him.

Military training would bust my chops. The process is brutal, cruel and humiliating. Only the most resilient survive; the weak are eliminated. The smallest infractions result in maximum punishment. I had left an ugly and desperate life behind, and I was not going back to the mean streets of Hyderabad.

Despite the harsh and unbearable conditions inside the academy, I was in heaven. I loved my seventeen course mates, including Mashood, the future alleged killer of General Zia. I would develop unbreakable bonds with a few of my badge mates, who will be my friends forever. The Air Force Academy was both transformative and grueling. It literally refined my being. I highly recommend it for all youth, especially the wayward ones.

PAF was extremely hard to get into. To graduate with wings? Forget it. Everyone and their dog wanted to be a fighter pilot. In my class alone, initially about 300 candidates applied. Three years later only thirteen graduated. Such was the rate of attrition. Under training, pilots could get pink slips. Reason: Unfit, period. No explanation, just pack your shit and get out. Unfit to serve, go, Get out!

I was not a team player and lacked officer-like qualities. Additionally, I was not good at following orders and usually got my badge mates in trouble. Flaying authority, taking shortcuts, being late, oversleeping, giggling, smiling, laughing too loud and all kinds of risk taking came natural to me. Taking shortcuts and not following rules would become a lifelong problem.

In the PAF academy I was flight trained by various flight instructors, including Air Commodore Shahid Khan, a handsome top gun and a highly decorated officer, whose sweet and kind guidance helped mold me into a tamed spirit. I looked up to him and emulated him. After a distinguished career, SK went on to become an inventor, a literary figure with a remarkable book, called 'E-Jihad.' Forty-five years later, I would bump into him on Facebook. SK graciously offered to write 'Foreword' for this book. A thorough gentleman!

After one well-deserved relegation—meaning demotion for six months—I barely graduated as a commissioned officer with an aeronautical degree. That was the happiest day of my life. Entering USA several years later would be my second.

My commanding officer, despite SK's assurances, had serious reservations about recommending me for graduation, and quite justifiably I may add. I pleaded with him and promised to be a responsible officer. Somehow, against his better judgment, he let me slide as I was a good stick, fearless, relentless and determined to persevere. I stood outside his office at attention for hours just so he could give me a chance to convince him. He was right, as the future would prove. I was not officer-like material. You can take the guy out of the ghetto, but you cannot take the ghetto out of the guy.

To my family & friends, I regret desecrating their country or their religion, which is a way of life for them. It's not my intention to insult or belittle anyone or anything in particular. My beef is with institutionalized philosophies and values. I have enormous respect and admiration for many on a personal level. I apologize if my writings have crossed lines of faith or impugned their beliefs. That is not my intent.

In 1972, I did my jet conversion course in Karachi, the financial capital of Pakistan, embroiled in ethnic and religious terrorism. Most of my family members live there.

After a difficult year in this port city, I got my posting orders to an MIG-19 fighter squadron. I absolutely loved flying fighters but hated the rest, gradually losing interest in the military. For every one hour of flying, I couldn't put up with the remaining 23 hours of pure shit, useless perks, salutes, titles and ranks. I wanted to play, chase girls and live a better life than I was living. The future looked bleak to me.

I served seven years in the military, getting disillusioned with the service. I scoffed at patriotic fervor. I would not be fulfilling my dad's dream after all. Nationalism, patriotism and any kind of flag waving bored the shit out of me. To unconditionally love one's country made no sense to me. I see such sentiments as divisive, naive and counterproductive to world peace and the camaraderie of human beings, The Oneness!

Pakistan was destined to be a failed state or, at best, one that would be teetering on the edge forever. Collapse seemed imminent. People seemed so ignorant, the system so corrupt and the future, hopeless. I wanted out. Out of the military and out of Pakistan. I was so fed up that I wanted out of the entire damn Eastern hemisphere.

I noticed how believers are so self-righteous; it's their way or the highway. The holy Book enshrines such self-proclaimed moral superiority and purity as compared to their fellow beings who may have other faiths or no faith.

In my world, the angel and the devil slept side by side peacefully. Well, to a large extent, although the devil was awake more, and the angel slept a lot. I am quite fortunate to have developed clarity on most significant issues we face in our daily lives. Freedom from religious dogmas and cultural, traditional and patriotic sentiments have done my thinking a world of good. I sincerely wish the same upon others.

I developed a strong desire to make my home in America. I despised living in Pakistan. I am not proud of my motherland. I am ashamed to be from Pakistan. Though I feel fortunate that I was raised there because growing up in a tough environment has steeled me to bear my burdens well and carry my crosses patiently. I retain the best of the East and mix it with the best of the West. No confusion, unlike many expats who have self-identity issues, living confused, muddled lives.

Just because you were born in a particular place on this vast planet, should that fact, which is beyond your control, obligate you to love, cherish and respect that geographical and political entity, unconditionally? Compel you to stay stuck within those boundaries? Absolute nonsense and not for me. I started planning to migrate to the United States, which I imagined was the land of sex, drugs and rock 'n roll. Boy, I was right.

I did not meet a white man until I was in my early twenties. I had just graduated from the PAF academy as an officer. I met the man in the bar of the officers' mess at the Karachi air basin 1972. He was an American fighter pilot, part of the U.S. Air Force squadron visiting on assignment. Pakistan and the United States had a defense pact, under which the two countries would participate in joint military exercises that involved MIG-19 fighters against F-4 phantom jets. I flew the Chinese made MIG, a crude, day-only, multiengine, supersonic fighter jet.

Flying the fucker was an experience words cannot define. It was OMG! The American and I talked about life in America for hours over drinks. He drank heavily; I was still a teetotaler. I was fascinated by the English speaking white American and was all ears, listening intently and absorbing things about life in America, the faraway land of milk and honey and scantily dressed chicks. It would be quite a contrast to the burqa-clad women on the men-only streets of my surroundings. Boy, I would kill to see a white woman in skimpy clothes. The very idea gave me wet dreams. My hormones were raging, and I had a perpetual hard-on, both physically and mentally.

I cultivated an eclectic, eccentric and electrifying mind and a healthy body with a good attitude. Though I was a sick puppy in need of sexual cure. I had blisters on my hand from excessive masturbation ... Smile. Let's not be so serious and so judgmental. Notice how only a few of us stay focused, listen carefully, absorb, reflect and then decide. Most people jump to half-assed conclusions with guns half cocked. Oh, there I go talking about cock. See, I warned you I was a sick puppy.

The PAF trains airmen, turning young punks into officers and fighter pilots. Pilots are under a contract to serve as long as they are deemed medically fit. Understandably, the PAF doesn't want to spend thousands of dollars on training pilots, only to have them leave the Air Force and join some airline. Pilots could not arbitrarily resign according to the terms of the contract. I was determined to leave. I figured they would have to throw me out. I didn't give a shit. Expel me, fuck you, get me out of this hellhole.

To make money, a fellow officer named Hani and I devised a scheme to cheat at cards. We were in cahoots with a shopkeeper who sold playing cards. We would buy a sealed package, unseal it, Mark the cards, repack them and give them back to the shopkeeper. When we went to his shop to buy cards, accompanied by the unsuspecting opposing players, the shopkeeper would sell us the same package we had marked. The rot has set in, corrupted to the core.

Then one night, we rented a hotel room in the swanky Hotel Intercontinental in Lahore and started the game, which lasted the better part of the night. This particular party kept losing thousands of rupees, hand after hand, on bets they would place. They assumed that the deck of cards had to be marked. They got suspicious as their losses defied logic. Suspecting foul play, the infuriated party threw the cards in the air and got up. Pulling out a gun, they called us on it. They bolted the hotel room door and called in backup. A professional card reader came and checked the cards, one by one, for markings while we held our breath, expecting trouble. Finally, to our relief, he threw his hands in the air, said "They are clean," and walked out of the room. They never played with us again.

We financed our lifestyle with our winnings as the air force pay was paltry. For a year or two, I was heavily involved in card games, raising enough cash to buy a motorbike and, later, an airline ticket abroad. How could I leave the service? I started to commit acts that would get me a discharge: brawling, disobeying and other acts unbecoming of an officer. They wouldn't let me go. I had to go for the last resort, the nuclear option. As I write, Pakistan and its nemesis, India, are actually thinking about using the nuclear option on each other. Such is the madness, despite warnings of utter chaos, killings, and total annihilation. Both sides are fighting over disputed land, called Kashmir, a princely state in the Himalayas.

The MIG-19 has a standard checklist that mandates that if, for any reason, the landing gear does not come down, the pilot is fucked. Pilots are instructed to declare an emergency, drop their fuel tanks in a safe area and eject. That's right, eject. That's a little harsh, don't you think? The Chinese engineers figured that landing a high performance MIG-19 on its belly at a high speed surely would cause combustion and turn the jet into a fireball when it hit the hot concrete runway.

Well, I thought that was an overreaction. A pilot shouldn't have to waste the aircraft and endanger his spinal cord by pulling the ejection handle. I needed to test that theory. It surely would get someone's attention.

One hot day, I went for the jugular. I took off on an air combat mission with SK as my leader. I managed my fuel flow so that on our return from a sortie, I had my fuel tanks close to empty. Timing went like clockwork.

G-suit drenched with sweat, I was about to pull a stunt no pilot ever had, in the history of the PAF. As I called Air Traffic Control (ATC) on the radio for landing clearance, both the fuel starvation lights lit up, one after the other. The gear unsafe horn (that automatically comes on, when landing gear is up below the landing speed) started buzzing loudly in my helmet, warning me of impending disaster unless I lowered the landing gear. It did not faze me. I was determined to get out of the service or die trying.

I sat calmly in the cockpit, focusing on making a textbook perfect landing. The officer in the control tower, who watches with binoculars for any such occurrence, screamed over his radio, warning me that my landing gear was up. "Go Around," screamed the ATC, repeatedly in my helmet. I ignored his order. He did not know that it was a planned maneuver by a kamikaze pilot. Desperate people do desperate things, and I was desperate to get the hell out of Dodge. Chicks and rock 'n roll were waiting for me in America. I was already late.

My perfect landing was about to reduce the multi-million dollar fighter jet to rubble. The Chinese manufacturers were right. Eject!

When the jet hit the sizzling hot runway, the impact started a slow-burning fire, but having no fuel, there was no explosion as the Chinese had feared. After a perfect touchdown, the MIG slid on her belly and came to a screeching halt. I took my helmet off and jumped out of the cockpit, calmly walked away from the burning jet. Like most young people, I felt indestructible and immortal. I didn't care if I died, either. Just give me the fucking pink slip

Life sucked, pretty much like it does for the poor bastard suicide bombers today. Bosses were confounded, why a competent pilot would do such a reckless and stupid thing? I was promptly grounded and put on a desk job - a life sentence to a fighter jock. An inquiry ensued.

During the interrogation, I was asked why I didn't go around when ordered to by ATC, to which I repeated a line I had read or made up, "Sir, I could not discern the command from the tower." When asked why not, my answer made the interviewer smile wryly. I said, "Sir, the gear unsafe warning horn was blowing so loud I could not hear the command to go round by ATC."

I faced a court martial. I was banned from flying and referred to a psychiatrist, then confined to barracks.

Baba Saeen came to my rescue. Instead of a court-martial, I was simply expelled. ***Dishonorable discharge*** was the term used by the service. Had it not been for family connections, which went to the top—the Bhutto clan—I still would be rotting in 'Bumfuck Egypt'. Life was miserable. I had no steady guide or elder to hold my hand and point me in the right direction. I needed cash ... pronto. In desperation, I asked my half-assed girlfriend, the Chief Minister's daughter, to help a brother out. I asked if she would marry me and get this nigga out of a jam. She understandably said, fuck no. Who wants to marry a loser?

I was desperate, dateless, jobless and homeless.

The year was 1975. I spent a few months riding around aimlessly on my motorcycle, feeling sorry for myself. My older brother, TG, helped me out as much as he could. He, too, was unhappy because his entertainment career was going nowhere. He wanted to be a movie star, but he was a bad actor, unwilling or unable to accept and change course. Some people just can't or won't change course. To them admitting error and taking responsibility is admitting failure, defeat. TG would slowly wither away.

I hated myself, my community and my country. Here I was in my twenties, in the prime of my life, young, dumb and full of cum. Something had to give. American movies held the promise of a better future. There was a colorful life somewhere as seen in technicolor Western movies. Now how do I get there?

I had to find a way soon.

5

UNITED KINGDOM

To get a U.S. visa was like winning the lottery. Everybody and their dog wanted to go to the United States. The USA is seen as a ticket to riches by young people around the globe and considered the 'shining light on top of the Hill.' President Reagan was right.

Out of the service, I bummed around, I didn't know how to get the hell out. My family wasn't too proud of me. One day I rode my Honda motorcycle to the United States Embassy in Karachi. Once in the Embassy, the Paki handler looked down on me as if I were a leper. I was given a date to come back. On the specified day, I returned to find a line longer than the last time. I waited for my turn, and finally my name was called. I calmly sat down with the interviewing American visa officer. He asked me why I wanted to go to the United States? I lied thru my teeth, gave him some lame excuses. He seemed unimpressed and knew I was lying. As expected, my request was promptly denied.

Not many young men left and returned. The visa section officers knew that and vetted the applicants accordingly. I was not ready to give up, never.

I saw poverty, filth, fear, despair and desperation everywhere. Swarms of unemployed roamed the streets. Disagreements between religious, tribal, cultural and linguistic factions often turned violent. It was no place for an upstanding, honest citizen like me, wink, wink!

I was a thief, a liar, and a cheat, but I had a conscience, a crook you could trust.

As soon I had enough funds, I took the first plane out of there. After a brief stopover in Damascus, Syria, the plane flew to France, which did not have a prior visa requirement to enter. I cleared immigration and customs at the Paris airport and checked into a seedy motel overnight. I had never seen so many white people in one place at the same time.

After clumsily hitting on French chicks, I took a train to see Mo, a former Air Force friend who was married to a boring Frenchwoman and living a dreary life in Strasbourg. I spent a couple of days with Mo. He was stuck in a dead end career, going nowhere. I didn't care for France as chicks weren't falling over each other to get to me, undermining my confidence. Language must be the barrier, I consoled myself. Unimpressed and disappointed with France, I left for the U.K and arrived at London's Heathrow Airport without a visa, but with hopes and dreams of grandeur and a fire in the belly, Dante's inferno!

The party and celebration of life were about to begin.

The U.K had a policy of issuing or denying visas on arrival, issuing discretionary visas, depending on who you were and why you wanted to enter the U.K. They routinely put South Asians on return flights to their countries of origin. I knew that, but I was willing to take a chance, a huge chance. Hey, I was willing to roll the imaginary dice. I didn't have much to lose.

Smartly dressed, well prepared, but with a trembling heart, I entered the immigration booth. I was like a duck, cool on the surface, but paddling like hell under the surface. The immigration official was about to make a beautiful mistake. The rookie would stamp my green passport with a six-month visitor's visa, taking my breath away. She had to be new at her job. Oh lord, these Caucasian chicks are driving me insane.

I was leaving the East behind, finally and thankfully, cutting the umbilical cord, forever. I was determined to make a successful life for myself in the West, Whatever it took. I did not know how but if anybody could, I would. Play it by ear, be open to the magic, beauty and fun of life. Opportunity had knocked at my door, and I was fully prepared to answer the knock and open the door to... Disneyland?

I did not have much money, but I was full of goodwill, ambition, a good work ethic (hammered into me by the military) plus a burning desire to make it. Dizzy with delight, I initially checked into a Lutheran hostel for students and spent the following few months doing odd jobs at various dance clubs and pubs, looking for a way to get to my dream world, USA.

I started having a fabulous time in London, overstaying my welcome. I began assisting and chauffeuring a wealthy, arrogant and traditional Desi bank owner. He was married to an actress Dad was banging in his heydays. They lived on the West End, a posh area of London. This seemingly pious banker, who did not drink or smoke, catered to shady African despots, wealthy Middle Eastern sheiks from Gulf States, Russian arms dealers, Eastern European smugglers and you name it. I was his driver, bodyguard and confidant for several months.

Desi parents are generally on the lookout for potential partners for their daughters. He was no exception. His bank would later merge with BCCI, the Bank of Credit and Commerce

International. I kept an account at his bank in London, near the bankers' street.

I was pleasantly surprised by and sold on the Western lifestyle. The people were law abiding and respectful of others. London was lovely. One day the banker secretly recorded my flirtatious telephone conversation with girls. I did not know telephone talks could be recorded. He became furious, pulled a gun and ordered me to get out of his house. He claimed I broke his trust. Hey, I was only trying to get laid. Jeez!

In London, I had met an attractive Dutch girl.

Eva was perhaps seventeen or barely eighteen, I never asked. We fell madly in love—my first with a westerner. We had a lovely romance for many months, making out and fondling, but no penetration. We were both virgins. I was singing and dancing 24/7. Then one night my elation ended. Eva caught me tipsy and making out on the dance floor with a stranger at the discotheque where I worked in Piccadilly Square. I had started drinking beer, frequently drank too much. She angrily, hysterically dumped me on the spot.

It was very heartbreaking and traumatizing. I tried every which way there was to get back with her, but she wanted none of it, smart girl. I showed up unannounced at her house on the outskirts of London, only to be sternly warned by her evil mother to leave them alone and that Eva didn't want to see me - ever again. I was very sad, crushed and devastated. I wept like a baby - for a day.

I did not do drugs, smoke or drink until I moved to the West. I was an adult virgin, having foolishly followed my father's advice to abstain from drinking, smoking and having sex until I was sufficiently grown. A big mistake. Lost out on years of fun. Elders' advice is not always right. We erroneously confuse seniority in age with superiority in wisdom. Not so. A stupid youngster will most likely become a stupid old fool. An ass in Lahore will be a bigger ass in London or Los Angeles (L.A.)

While in London, I worked for several night clubs illegally without a 'Green card,' getting fired from almost every one of them for various infractions, mostly involving booze and women. To be honest, I think I may have been fired from most jobs I have had in my life. That probably was instrumental in my decision to work for myself later on. I guess I was not built to be an employee. Like most employees, I must have thought I was smarter than my employers and that I knew how to run their businesses better than they did, a common affliction with most employees. I am best suited to working alone, by myself, for myself. I work well with others on a case-by-case basis, networking and making temporary alliances. Teamwork!

I had taken a swan dive into the untested waters of British nightlife. What a difference from the miserable and barren life I had left behind. London was unbelievable. I had died and gone to heaven. I was born in the wrong part of the globe, gods had made an error, I was certain. I had my first drink and first sexual experience in London. I lost my virginity to a Jamaican English whore in a dingy Soho motel. It was a nasty first. I went down on the Jamaican and stayed there, thinking that maybe kitty is supposed to smell like that. Even the call girl was disgusted. Imagine that. I did not go down on a woman for a long time after that nasty experience. Eew! There is nothing that smells worse than a stinky kitty.

I spent a very exciting year or so in London, often working and partying eighteen hours a day, seven days a week. I had never seen so many available white girls. I was so ecstatic, living the high life in the fast lane. I literally felt on top of the world. Then one day I saw an ad in *The Times*. Promoters were looking for volunteers to pool money and hire a charter jet to go to New York city to see Paul McCartney and the Wings in concert at Madison Square Gardens. I replied to the ad and to my huge surprise, the organizers scored me a visa to America from the U.S. Embassy in London. How fucking incredible, I mused.

My previous encounter with the U.S. embassy in Karachi must not have showed up in the computer. They were going to let me into the United States of America, Really?

I went to the bank, closed my account and then wrote a bad check to pay for the trip to New York. Hallelujah. I took a taxi to Heathrow Airport. Trembling inside, I checked in with immigration control expecting to be denied boarding. I was allowed to board a chartered flight, to the heavens. My parting present to the pious banker was a check for £1,200 that was going to bounce. Bastard pulled a gun on me.

Notice how the religious beliefs and cultural mores make most righteous people stupid and dangerous.

6

ENTERING PARADISE

I N July of 1976, I arrived in New York city on a 7-day visitor's visa. With a cool demeanor, but a pounding heart, I cleared the immigration and customs booth. I was shocked, I was actually in the United States and it was not a dream. It was one of the happiest and most exciting days of my life, second Only to my graduation as a pilot in 1972. I was beyond joy, in a delightful daze. I had $1,800 on me. I felt I had plenty. New york, was unbelievable to this wanderer. My neck cramped as I looked up at the skyscrapers, marveling at the wonders of engineering. I felt as if I was floating in the air, walking on water. "Wild horses couldn't drag me away" to quote Mick Jaeger, vowing never to return. Never. Are you kidding me? Not in a million years. Would you?

I had come home.

After a few days of sightseeing in New York, we went to see a concert. That's one time I was not interested in music. Paul was okay, but I was busy plotting my next move. After the concert, we planned to check out of our hotel and meet at LaGuardia Airport to fly back to London. The charter jet back to London would have an empty seat. I was going to take a slight detour. Instead of going to the airport, I took a taxi to the Greyhound bus terminal.

America was celebrating its bicentennial. I bought a one-way bus ticket to L.A., where I was going to look up an old acquaintance, Reeno, whose father was a powerful minister in the Sindh cabinet. I was friends with his half-sister in Karachi. We were lovers without sex for a few years, not too uncommon with Paki couples.

America welcomed me with open arms (and legs) right away. I met an attractive young girl on the bus. She was headed to Reno, Nevada. I started chit chatting and charmed her into doing something she said she had never done before. Neither had this hound. As the night fell, I had my first sexual experience in America, in total darkness, on the backseat of a Greyhound bus, passing through Oklahoma. It blew me away. Does this happen every day in America? I was delirious. I ended up in Reno making out with her throughout the long trip. Oh, how I did not want the three-day journey to end.

I hitchhiked to L.A., the City of Angels. I was fascinated by the hustle and bustle, the multitude of cars, the freeways, open airspace and the weather. This will be home, I swore. McDonald's food would be delicious for years to come. Hitchhiking would be the mode of transportation (meet people, get laid.) Initially, I stayed with Reeno, got a job in the parts department of Gunnell Aviation at the Santa Monica Airport. I made friends with the owner's fun loving son. Bill was my age, a fellow rocker, and a skirt chaser. We were good friends for a few years. He helped me distinguish a nice ass from a fat one. Smiles.

Bill would take me around and show me what a fine ass is - say, as supposed to an out of shape, big booty. He would point out the finer things of life to me, "Hey, Paki, pay attention, look at my sister's ass over there. See how round, proportional and insane her buns are. Now look at Linda, the girl behind the counter, notice how fat and disproportional her ass is. You got to pay attention to asses, Paki." **This was America,** I was wide-eyed.

I had no car, so I walked everywhere. I noticed that nobody walks in L.A. Soon I found a room for rent for $100 a month, moving in with a Thai family near Santa Monica airport. The Thai woman and her young daughter graciously took me in. The woman wanted me, but I wanted her teenage daughter, who was into cholos. Teens are fair game where I hailed from, but jailbait in the States. I would have to readjust, re-calibrate. I got a second, more exciting job driving a yellow cab at night.

I hung out in the Venice Beach area and became part of the local scene by the world famous Muscle Beach. I did whatever it took to make money, and, importantly, to get laid and to not get caught by the Immigration and Naturalization Service.

Venice Beach is a unique place. Going there is like a pilgrimage for me. I rented a room on Brooks avenue. When I was not flirting, I was selling marijuana, coke, mushrooms and Quaaludes. Anything you wanted, I either had it in stock or I could get it with a phone call. Hitting on girls was my number one goal in life. I was horny all the time. Beautiful women drove me insane. I was worse than a kid in a candy store. Imagine having come from living in misery in Pakistan to Venice Beach, the pussy capital of the world. I was so thankful for everything, to be alive, healthy, so grateful for America.

The boardwalk on Venice Beach was, and still is, a wild place with a variant tapestry of human beings. You saw all kinds of people there, all sorts of incredibly gifted people: musicians, magicians, painters, comedians, Hare Krishna drum beaters and talented artsy-folksy people. Blacks, whites, Mexicans and brown people (local lingo we called them brothers, honkies, Chicanos, and rag heads, to be cool :)

I soon had money to buy a used Toyota, thank you America. I moved in with Gunnells for a while and became part of the family. We were all happy campers. Mrs. Gunnell had a wayward daughter, Bobby, she hoped Bobby and this nice young immigrant man would hook up. Bobby said 'no way.' I noticed that the people who live the most fulfilling lives are the ones who are always rejoicing at what they have and not what they don't. Self-acceptance has to be way up there in the hierarchy of factors that govern happiness and contentment.

I had the telephone number of a former Air Force acquaintance named Sam who lived in West Covina. One day I called him up - and boom - Sam became my lifelong friend. He is an amazing man- eccentric, very playful and the weirdest man you will ever meet. Sam brightens people's lives, wherever he goes. He has enriched my life in so many ways, and I already owe him gratitude beyond any words or acts. What the bastard lacks in looks, he makes up with his colorful and jovial personality. We had the time of our lives running wild in the streets of Hollywood. He worked for Sparkletts, delivering water to homes, charming housewives and getting them into bed while their men were out working. The man was frequently scoring, making me jealous. I hated him. We often would double up and party.

My dear, buddy Sam is a horny animal, and I have seen him perform. One time, he picked up a girl driving on Interstate 10 east of L.A. He brought her home, told me to watch the show and started banging her right in front of me. His sessions lasted hours as opposed to mine. I had trouble with premature ejaculation. An uncle who fancied himself as an herbal doctor would wrap my tool in a homeopathic supplement consisting of ginkgo, ginseng, and Echinacea. Did it help? Fuck no. I am glad my ex had me as a lover exclusively or else she would sell me out.

While Sam was in bed with her, performing like a stud, I went for the jugular - her purse, plucked her credit card and hurried out to use the card in various stores. I charged small stuff here and there until the Iraqi clerk at a liquor store got suspicious and called the police. I got out of there fast and raced to my car, parked around the block. I must not have stood out, as in rough neighborhoods many people are running.

Sam later moved to Honolulu, which was to become my playground. Sam raised two bright sons, one of whom works for the spy agency in D.C., perhaps coordinating drone attacks in Pakistan. Who knows? Sam had an arranged marriage in Pakistan. His wife and I became good friends. Sam's marriage ended twenty-five years later, which surprised me as I thought they were happy together. Some people just keep shit secret. I know of few more couples that I thought were happy, who abruptly divorced. WTF!

The taxicab business suited me just fine. I got to see L.A. like no other. I had very little, but I was happy, perhaps the happiest I have ever been. I've practiced the art of living with less all my life, as opposed to my spouse, who wanted to live large, creating major divisions. I also noticed that you won't be happy with more until you're happy with less.

I would strike up conversations with my cab fares, taking them to their destinations by the longest route possible. One time at LAX, I picked up a fare who told me to take him to Beverly Hills. He looked familiar. While driving, I looked in the rearview mirror, and who did I see, but a scowling Paul Newman, my favorite star from the movie *Butch Cassidy and the Sundance Kid*. I am not much of a star worshipper—the type who wants autographs for their son and shit—but I was interested. I tried to humor him. "Hey Butch, what's up, man?" Butch was uninterested. He was quiet and aloof. He must have been having a bad hair day. He might as well have said " Just shut up and drive, rag head."

While driving taxi in Hollywood, I hooked up with a drug ring led by Charlie, an East Coast transplant with blue eyes. They were selling drugs on the street. They recruited me, and I started slinging at LAX, peddling marijuana to fellow drivers, clients, whomever. Charlie would give me a pound at a time, which, on his instruction, I would keep in the trunk of the taxicab. If I were busted, I could claim that it did not belong to me—plausible deniability—and say some passenger must have left behind. Passengers occasionally did leave stuff behind that I never returned. I got involved in the gang's other activities: pimping, stealing, credit card fraud and all sorts of petty crime. Small time petty crooks.

One night around midnight, when I was driving a yellow cab, I dropped off a fare south of LAX in Torrance and started racing with another car on the Sepulveda Boulevard. A motorcycle cop snuck up alongside my cab and signaled me to pull over. Shit, I was in trouble. Then the cop sped up to the other racer and pulled him over too. Damn it, I couldn't get a ticket; the cab company would fire me. What to do?

After pulling us over, the cop parked his bike approximately 50 feet ahead of me, behind the other car. An officer came over to my driver's side. I had my window rolled down. He said, "Sir, you know why I pulled you over. License and registration, please." I reached for the registration in the glove compartment. The officer said, "Stay right here, Sir. I will be back shortly." He walked over to the other racer. On a panicked whim, I made an executive decision, a sorry one. The previous day, I had seen **Bullet**, a great movie with Steve McQueen in it. The movie had a gnarly car race scene.

I turned the headlights off and floored the gas pedal and took off at full speed ahead, leaving the shocked police officer in my wake. I zigzagged through South-central L.A. - whose streets I knew fairly well. Speeding through rough neighborhoods like a bullet, I saw no sign of the officer in my rearview mirror. I took a victorious sigh of relief. Had I just pulled off the Great Escape? Hardly.

I relaxed, turned on the headlights and went back to cruising the dark and vacant streets, humming to soothe my frayed nerves. All of a sudden, I saw red, blue and yellow lights everywhere. Several squad cars descended on me, with sirens wailing. A helicopter with a searchlight circled overhead. The motorcycle cop had called in backup.

The cops had found me by spotting the dome light on the cab's roof. The dome light stays on, indicating the cab is available for hire; it goes off when the meter is turned on. In my haste to get away, I had totally forgotten to turn the meter on.

I found myself in a world of trouble as every squad car had been following the dome light. I stuck out like a sore thumb. They encircled me, blocking my cab with a squad car. I was ordered out of the cab, roughly thrown against the vehicle and frisked. Then the motorcycle cop thrashed my wiseass. He threw me on the ground, and then five or six cops beat me to a pulp (like Rodney King) led by Officer Durger.

I was black and blue, but being illegal and at fault, I had no alternative but to put my tail between my legs and accept the consequences of my actions. I spent a cold night in jail. I lost my job, my pride, few broken ribs to boot. I remembered the name of the motorcycle cop who had caused most of my humiliation, and I knew that he lived around Manhattan Beach. The badass in me thought about going after the officer, but as my injuries healed, my vindictiveness faded. I was just glad not to get deported. After that incident, whenever officer Durger saw me, the bastard would give me an evil smile. I had been out of line. It's always good to accept responsibility and not point fingers at others.

I was fired from Yellow Cab. No problem. I got a job with Red Cab in Hollywood, lying on the application, of course, not telling them about my firing. I made contacts with street girls on Hollywood boulevard and with gay boys on Santa Monica Boulevard. Providing ganja, girls and boys, to customers became my side business. I would network and hook them up, getting my cut, mostly in cash, but in sexual favors too. I spent many nights cruising the boulevard at night and scoring temporary trysts of erotic nature, frequently getting blowjobs on dimly lit side streets and in secluded alleys. Hallelujah, praise the Lord. USA, USA!

It was all fun and games, but I was restless. I soon engineered plans to fly marijuana from Florida to California and distribute it to other states in rented airplanes that I would pilot. There are several ways to make one's immigration status legal; marriage to a U.S. citizen is the most popular one. The second best way is to invest in a legitimate business and create jobs. Then there are work-sponsored visas and student visas. How could I become an American citizen? The thought hounded me. I had to find a way to become legal.

I seriously considered starting a flight school, but the drug business seemed more lucrative. Soon—being master of the obvious—I discovered that, chances of survival are slim. If the police don't get you, one of your own will. Few survive the vicious circle.

I hung out with Joey. He was a school dropout, a fun loving chick magnet. We chased girls, sold drugs and partied in L.A.'s trendy Manhattan Beach. My homie Joey was a good man, street smart and clever. In my haste to get rich, I set up a sting operation that would come back to haunt me big time.

The sting went like this: Three members of Charlie's gang and I went to Miami to make a marijuana buy from a Colombian contact of Charlie's. They had $35,000 cash to make a purchase. We checked into a motel and waited for the Colombian seller. There is endless waiting in the drug trade, similar to police surveillance. At a given time, when I went out with a ring member to get fast food from a Taco Bell, I went to a pay phone and secretly telephoned Joey's brother, who was standing by with a friend. They rushed to the motel and stormed the room, wearing Drug Enforcement Agency (DEA) garb and brandishing fake guns. They cuffed the two stunned gang members, threw them face down on the floor, searched the room, grabbed the money and got out of there fast.

Shortly afterward, the third ring member and I returned with tacos. I pretended to be shocked at the assault and helped the 'victims' off the floor, feigning anger and surprise. They were stumped; who knew? Joey and I had planned to split the loot. They did a great job of robbing the bad guys but then ... my crime partner disappeared with the cash. I have never seen him since. I thought there was honor among thieves. Wrong. Well, I have to come clean since this is a factual autobiography. My bad.

A few days earlier, I had done something screwy with good intentions, but it blew up on me. I have to admit to a faux pas, and you Are going to hate me for this.

Joey had a beautiful dog, a German shepherd named Gizmo, whom he had for years, and he absolutely adored that animal. Gizmo was the first dog I ever petted, to please my homie. The culture I grew up in did not recognize animals as pets. In Pakistan, animals, mainly dogs and cats, live out on the streets, not in homes. When we saw animals, we shooed them away or threw rocks at them. We didn't cuddle them or even Touch them. Many of these animals were wild and had rabies. A couple of my friends had died after being bitten by a rabid animal. Later, I learned that, in the West, the bond between a dog and their owner is hugely important. The dog often becomes the master's best friend and in some cases, a substitute child. I did not know that back then.

In my infinite wisdom, I thought that Gizmo was always in the way of our plans, a liability stopping Joey from doing better things. We couldn't go away longer than several hours because Gizmo had to be taken care of- and rightly so. We couldn't go out of town for business or pleasure because of Gizmo. I am ashamed of what I did next.

One day while Joey was out driving a cab, I entered his house, or should I say, I broke into his pad. I called for Gizmo. Instead of barking, he came up to me with his tail wagging, to greet the master's best friend. I said, "Hey Gizmo, come on, you want to go for a ride? Let's go for a ride." He jumped at the chance, followed me to my vehicle and hopped into the bed of my pickup. I planned to take him fifty or sixty miles away, to an area from where he could not find his way home. Heartless?

I drove to east L.A, stopped the pickup by a park in a sparsely populated neighborhood and let Gizmo out. The dog was happier than a clam because I had taken him for a long ride which I seldom did. Gesturing him to run, I said, "Run, Gizmo, run." He hesitated. Then he was really confused when he saw me jump into the pickup and take off. Watching Gizmo running after me in the rear view mirror was a little heartbreaking, even for me. But I consoled myself that I was doing the dirty job for my friend's greater good. I left Gizmo miles away from home, thinking I had done the right thing, helping a friend do better things. Someone else will love the pet.

To my surprise and dismay, Joey was heartbroken when he discovered Gizmo was missing. I thought he would forget about the dog, get another one and move on. After all, it was just a dog, not his child. Joey and I put up posters in several neighborhoods. He called out Gizmo's name repeatedly until he was hoarse. I saw Joey sobbing. He wasn't eating or sleeping properly. All this time, I was feeling terribly guilty. I realized I had blundered, but I could not tell him the truth. I drove back to where I had left Gizmo to see if I could find him and bring the dog back. My friend suspected me, occasionally asking me to please own up. He thought I could have taken Gizmo for a joyride, and his beloved dog could have fallen or jumped out of my pickup accidentally.

He suspected me, and I think that's why he took off with the loot after robbing the bad guys in Miami. He may have told Charlie that I set them up.

I was the prime suspect in the Miami sting. I knew too much about the gang's activities. They were On to me. Charlie decided to kill me. They devised a plan and hired John, a tall good looking vicious hit man, who would do a messy job later. As part of the plan, John befriended me and waited for the right opportunity.

One evening, I contacted one of Charlie's drug sources and bought twenty-five pounds of weed from him. I was going to retail it on the street in L.A., tripling, quadrupling my investment. Charlie found out that I had gone around him and made the purchase, which in the drug business, is a gross violation. You do not contact another dealer's source. Dealers jealously guard their sources. The source is money, where trust is cultivated over time. There are undercover cops and snitches everywhere. Charlie must have been furious. He conspired to rob me of my load of ganja and call in a hit. Charlie called me up and said that he had a celebrity buyer who wanted to buy all my stash at an attractive price.

Under the lure of this sweet deal, I was set up in the Malibu hills, where an actor supposedly would buy all my stash. I smelled a rat. The deal was too good to be true. We all know what that means ... If the deal is too good to be true, it probably is. I was unfazed. I loved danger. Bring it on.

It was a moonless night, pitch dark. John, the hit man, and I met an hour before midnight at the Horseshoe saloon on highway 101 in Malibu. I was supposedly carrying twenty-five pounds of my life savings in marijuana. Hey, that was 25 times $500 or $125000. That was a ton of dough. We had a drink at the bar and made some awkward small talk. John was shifty, impatient and acting suspicious, but it did not bother me. I was stupidly brave and totally fearless regarding the potential danger. I loved the excitement. My adrenalin was running sky high.

The hit man suggested that we light up a joint in the parking lot and then ride up to the Malibu hills together in his white Porsche. He said I could leave my vehicle in the saloon parking lot and transfer the stuff to his car. I was carrying two suitcases, supposedly containing the stash. Since I suspected foul play, I had played cute and replaced the pot with junk—shoes, clothes, and other stuff. If I were being set up, someone would try to rip me off like I had done to them in Miami. Fine, let them take the junk in the suitcases. I figured If I were wrong and there was a genuine buyer, I would apologize and go back to get the real stuff, which I had left behind in my house on 39th Street in Manhattan Beach, where I was rooming with Bill and his future bride. Prisons are full of inmates, who thought they had all things covered.

A weird thing occurred earlier that fateful day. I was driving home in my pickup, cruising along the ocean in Playa del Rey, happily heading towards my pad, singing and dancing to L.A.'s great radio stations. I saw a Harley bike rider ahead clad in a full leather outfit. He was making crazy S-turns at a high speed. Suddenly, he slipped and crashed right in front of me. Holy shit. I stopped my vehicle and, like any good samaritan, rushed over to help him. Too late. He had struck his head on the pavement. The biker lay motionless, bleeding, perhaps dead? The dead or dying biker had a switchblade knife on his belt. My larcenous heart wanted the knife. Instinct? Good fortune, as I was to find out later that night.

The stolen knife would save my life in the next few hours. Cars buzzed by without stopping. People are always in a hurry to get home after a day's work. I looked around; nobody was watching. I quickly relieved the dead biker of his knife—and his wallet. I didn't think he would need them anymore, I would. I don't carry any kind of weapon, however, that evening at the last minute, after packing the suitcases with junk, I noticed the lone knife laying on the dresser. On a hunch, I slipped the biker's stolen knife into my jacket, just in case someone wanted to rip me off. They better not, as I am a badass ... a fiendish Smile.

Back to Malibu.

The hit man and I got into his Porsche and drove up to this spacious mansion in the hills in total darkness. John parked the car a short distance from this mansion and asked me to grab the stash. "Let's roll," he said in a hushed voice. Those would be his last words.

A quiet suspense in the air, it was pitch dark. I got out of the car carrying a suitcase in each hand. John came around to my side; I thought he was going to give me a hand with the suitcases. Instead, he slammed me with a crowbar that he had concealed in his right arm. All I saw was his arm go up and smack me in the middle of my head. I was stunned by the severity and shock of the painful blow. Motherfucker!

Blood poured down my face, blinding me. I staggered and fell, dropping the suitcases. In that split second, I realized I was going down. This was a hit; John was going to kill me. They were wise to my trick in Miami. It was do or die. I thought about the knife. My hand instinctively reached into my pocket for the bikers knife. I tried opening the blade but couldn't find the button. Panicking, I tried to manually open the knife with both hands, cutting my own finger and thumb tendons. John came at me again with the crowbar raised over his head. I fended him off with the sharp blade, knifing my attacker multiple times.

John pulled a gun out of his pocket and shot me point blank. The shot missed me by a cunt hair. A miss is as good as a mile. John had his jugular vein cut. I didn't mean to slice him. I found out later, from the police report, that he had received eighty-two cuts on his body, all in a few seconds. After knifing him, I ran from the scene with blood streaming out of my head and hands, blurring my vision.

Bleeding profusely, John would stagger to his Porsche. Holding his throat with one hand, he had managed to start the vehicle and then bled to death in the Porsche. The engine was idling with John's head slumped over the steering wheel, when police arrived later, a grisly scene.

Two dead men within hours of each other? What in the hell, had I gotten myself into. I staggered to a nearby house and knocked on the door, barely able to stand, with a bloody knife still in my hand and the face and clothing drenched with blood. Military training had come in handy, but I was critically wounded. A woman living in that home had heard the scuffle, the gunshot and had already called 911. I was sure that these were my last moments on earth and that this woman would be my last to fondle. I was thinking sex, such was my state of mind.

While the poor woman was trying to stabilize me, I wanted to keep me from passing out, I kept touching her breasts and smiling in a chauvinistic, lecherous way, puzzling the confounded woman. This lady had a look of disbelief on her face. Who would do that? The bloody knife had fallen from my hand, I lay on the floor with my head on her lap, listening to her soft anguished sobs, my face in her breasts, ah! what sweet end.

The paramedics and police soon arrived putting me on a stretcher and rushing to the hospital, in serious condition, with multiple wounds to my head and hands. I needed forty stitches in the center of my head, thumb tendons stitched and needed a blood transfusion. I did not know what condition John was in.

Around 5 a.m., as I lay in the hospital bed, drugged up with head and hands bandaged, two detectives walked in and introduced themselves, "I am homicide detective… and this is my partner, homicide detective…" I felt earth moved under my hospital bed when I heard the word 'Homicide.' I knew I was in a world of trouble. The detectives interviewed me, informing me that I had just killed a man. I had stabbed my companion numerous times. Adios freedom.

I was moved to the hospital ward of the L.A. County Jail on suspicion of murder. The atmosphere was hellish in there; it was a human zoo for wild animals. One negro inmate kept coming at me, claiming I was Jesus Christ Superstar, and the bastard wanted to suck my dick. I had to shoo him away several times, even calling the guard. I met an older criminal who had dysentery in his mouth, kept repeating, "Hey kiddo, it is a rat race, and remember, even if you win the rat race, you are still a rat." I nodded to be polite. He would walk away, laughing.

The detectives interrogated me for several days, conducting a thorough background investigation and checking up on my story, they knew I was telling the truth. I was defending myself, and I did not plan or intend to kill John. Surprisingly, I had not broken any laws. There were no drugs involved. They told me they would recommend that I not be charged. The detectives said it would be up to the D.A. to decide whether to prosecute.

15 days later, I was taken to the Santa Monica courthouse in chains, not knowing my fate.

I sat there wondering what was going on, waiting for my future to be decided by a scowling judge. My name was called in. I was worried sick, disheveled and in enormous pain. I couldn't believe my ears when I heard the D.A. tell the judge, "Your Honor, the people do not want to prosecute the defendant as it was clearly a case of self-defense." I had been attacked first; I merely defended myself, accidentally killing my attacker.

It turned out that John was a wanted man in few other states for several crimes, including murder. Numerous fake identifications were found on him, and the Porsche too was stolen. The judge addressed me, mutilating my last name, which is not easy to pronounce, neither was first or the middle.

He somberly said "Mr. Iktidyar Mestaaha Gaajnaabi, hope I'm pronouncing it right. D.A. tells me that… in the case of State of California vs. Gaajabee, it was a case of self-defense. The state declines to charge the defendant." Then he lowered his glasses and politely continued, "Therefore you are free to go home sir. You have no more business with my courtroom. I don't want to see you again in my courtroom…Next…"

A lightning bolt struck. I was in utter shock. Freedom, my heart wept with joy of gratitude. I was sold on the American legal system.

The gods were smiling on me. A brown man stabs a caucasian American to death and the American justice system acquits the Pakistani killer. USA, USA, USA!

My then, on again, off again girlfriend, Nancy, was there in the courtroom to take me home, sweet home. My stash of twenty-five pounds of marijuana was in the attic; safe. I always carried few telephone numbers of public phones handy in my little black book. If I was ever caught in a situation, my reply would be that when I had a customer who wanted to buy a big stash, I called that number. My contacts wanted to remain anonymous. They always contacted me.

The following day, the ring member called and said that the boss wanted to see me. He asked me to meet Charlie at a nearby bar.

Not kosher. I hurried to Toys R Us, bought a toy gun, concealed it in my jacket and met three of them at that busy bar in Manhattan Beach. I sat at a small table, facing Charlie with two of his hoodlums on his sides, my toy gun conspicuously visible.

Charlie was friendly, pretended that he was shocked, and asked what had happened between John and me. I told Charlie to cut the bullshit; I knew he was behind the attempt to snuff me out. I made it obvious that I had a gun on me, and—copying Charles Bronson in his vendetta movies—I threatened to go after them, one by one, and kill them. I didn't mean any of this of course. I was just bluffing, hoping that they would take me seriously and leave me alone. Well, they did.

They looked at each other with fear and must have taken my threat seriously. Charlie abruptly got up and left the table, hoodlums in toe. I found out later that they all had disappeared after our chat. They must have assumed I was coming after them; after all, I had just killed their tough guy. I drove by to see if they were still around. Their homes were padlocked. Every one of them was gone, perhaps back to the East Coast. Too much heat on the West Coast. A mad Paki was on the loose, gunning for them.

I never saw them again. I was not charged with any other offense. No one questioned my legal status. I was told that DEA would be contacting me, if they needed anything from me, they never did. The nightmare was over. However, I was always looking over my shoulder, afraid that they still might come after me—not a comfy feeling.

I feared the INS must want my ass out of the States. It didn't happen as I fell through the cracks. Praise Allah or whoever for the divine intervention.

7

PUERTO RICO

NANCY, the dark haired Italian hottie from New Jersey, had come to court to support me and take me home. I was glad to have her there. However, I was also dating a sweet eighteen-year-old, Judy—a brunette peach from Georgia—whom I had met at Venice Beach. Judy was from an upscale Atlanta family. She had moved to L.A., leaving her wealthy drug dealer fiancé behind in Atlanta.

These were the seventies, a decade of decadence, peace, love, sex, and drugs. Judy had run away to Hollywood to 'find her-self' and make sure that she wanted to settle down in the South. Because of my tendon injury, when Nancy and I got back from the courthouse, I couldn't wash or bathe myself. Judy and Nancy met each other awkwardly at my beach pad. They fought over - listen to this - they fought over as to who would soap and shower me. It was a comical scene. They put me on the spot by asking me to make that silly choice. Who wants to bathe this playboy? You believe that shit?

There I was a few hours ago, sitting in an awful jailhouse, shooing away a brother, who thought I was Jesus and that he had to suck my dick. I thought that my life was fucked, and then, several hours later, I had two hotties literally fighting over the right to shower me. Praise Allah. Ohm! Sheepishly, I voted for Judy. Nancy got very mad and stomped out of my place in a hissy fit. The Southern Belle barely won. I never saw Nancy again.

Judy and I hung out at the Venice beach, smoking pot, getting high, snorting coke and doing Quaaludes. We became inseparable. She asked me why I was so stressed out. I ought to be relieved, happy. I told her that I probably was going to be deported. I presumed that the authorities surely would put two and two together. They would find out about my status and deport me. Luckily, the right hand didn't know what the left was doing. Uncle Sam gave me a break. Judy swore that she wouldn't let that happen. How could she help her rag head friend stay in the States? I told her the only way was if I got married to an American. The sweet, innocent run away immediately suggested that we marry and play house. "I love you," she meant it.

Hmm, not a bad idea at all. I did, after all, like her a lot. I thought I should give it a shot. Who knows, maybe we could make it work. There was no downside, although she warned me that the violent boyfriend she left behind might show up. I didn't care. Violence was my middle name. No fear!

Judy married me in Las Vegas. We fell in love, or maybe lust, briefly, and lived together for a while, cognizant of the fact that it was a temporary relationship as she someday could move back to Georgia and marry her fiancé. I was not the marrying type, anyway. Although I was bruised, bandaged and not yet recovered from my fight. I limped to the courthouse to say our vows. On the steps of the courthouse, I felt totally in love with and indebted to her for helping me, loving me.

Judy was easy going, playful and had this beautiful habit of making love in strange, unlikely places and climaxing quickly, like birds do. That was quite a turn on for me, "Birdie, birdie,

60

cum" I would tease her. We were a great match sexually. We both came prematurely. She was an erotic and affectionate woman and I was insanely into sex, not kidding.

In 1978, I met Lynn, a midwestern blonde, at a dance club in the San Fernando Valley. I used to go dancing every evening, exploring new night clubs in the L.A. area and, of course, meeting girls. Dancing has always been my thing. My daily routine revolved around dancing. I couldn't wait for the work day to end so that I could go home, clean up, spray on some perfume, comb my hair, look in the mirror and say, "You handsome devil you," and go out to some club. I was in love with life.

I approached Lynn, strutting like Don Juan, the legendary hypersexual fictional character. I was about to meet my next girlfriend. "Would you like to dance?" I asked romantically. After some hesitation, she looked over to her girlfriend dancing on the floor, who gestured her to go. She said, "Okay." We danced and kissed and caressed on the dance floor. Wow, I couldn't believe my luck.

That evening, I took her home, we became lovers. In those days, it was relatively easy to get laid on the same night you met. I believe it was the first ever for her. No fear or knowledge of AIDS back then.

Afraid of retribution from Charlie's gang and for the love of flying, I wanted to go away, someplace far away. I solicited a job offer from an air taxi company in San Juan, Puerto Rico, thousands of miles away. The airline I would fly for, Dorado Wings, was owned by an elite resort called Little Dix Bay, located in Virgin Gorda, a magical tiny island, part of the British Virgin Islands. I was hired to fly BN-2A Islanders that carried nine passengers and a pilot. I flew tourists between the islands east of Puerto Rico to Barbados, stopping at St. Thomas, Tortola, Virgin Gorda and few other islands. I invited Lynn to join me in Dorado beach, on the outskirts of San Juan, once I give the green.

I lived like a Casanova, partying with tourists, along with having my live-in girlfriend Lynn at home. Wealthy tourists in party mode were easy to prey on. It was a great job, and I had a blast. I was barely making $800 a month, but I was flying and getting laid by different girls regularly. Flying and fucking were my number one priority then.

My elder brother by four years, Meesna, a sweet, simple and humble man, visited me in San Juan and was disappointed with my lifestyle. He thought I was working at a dead-end job and going nowhere. He pleaded with me to come back to Pakistan and join him in our hotel business. The five-story Ghaznavi Hotel was a landmark in downtown Hyderabad that Dad built in 1958. Meesna was the family patriarch and ran the household as my oldest brother, KG did not want to participate in the family business.

KG had a cushy job with the government, and he was content. The job had perks that included bribery and influence peddling. KG is hot-tempered, a strict disciplinarian, but also a principled man. He is married to one of our distant cousins, with whom he never got along. He ran his home with an iron hand, everyone knew who was the boss around. They have three handsome and productive sons. One of his sons lives in L.A, whom I adore. I have several family members in the L.A. area.

KG is small in physique, but big in ego with a colorful personality. He is a very funny, fun loving and hospitable fellow, who loves throwing parties, drinking, dancing and smoking cigars. I have always been fond of KG, and I put him on a higher pedestal. In 2001, he borrowed $20,000 from me as he had some financial difficulties. He solemnly promised to return my money in six months with interest. My brother, whom I held in high esteem, never returned the money, disappointing me. As collateral, KG gave me some worthless property papers, that I couldn't even wipe my ass with.

It taught me Not to lend money to family or friends. Not did I lose my money, I also lost respect for KG (cagey?) Now in all sincerity, I have to labor hard to stay friendly and be good to him. Pakistani culture mandates that elders of the family be respected. I also gave a loan of $6000 to one of the family members to bail her out. She promised but never returned it either. Another cousin in LA also ripped me off of $10k. List of grievances is long. How's that for dirty laundry? It would be understandable if you don't have it, but to have access and then not return my cash is downright dirty, not kosher. Wouldn't you agree? Just cause I was once a shameless thief growing up in Pakistan, You don't have to pull the same dacoity on me (haven't you heard I am disabled and need cash. And it's my cash.) Oh well...

I thanked Meesna and told him that I was very happy and that the life of poverty suited me just fine. Hey, I was young, dumb and full of cum. Nothing mattered but flying and fun. Tourists and flying were my world, and I was content.

However, I felt a strong change occurring within me - a paradigm shift. In my fuzzy, haphazard scheme of things, I was restless, searching for my place under the sun.

The visit from my brother perhaps triggered something within me, an ignition? He may have unconsciously challenged me to be my best and to do better than my loser life in PR. The very idea of gaining respect and honor intrigued me. After living a disgraceful life, I wanted to be respectable, yesterday!

I am going to take readers on a roller coaster ride ahead as I will be going through tumultuous changes. Stay with me and fasten your seat belts for a bumpy ride ahead. Let me share with you, as it can be done, I have lived long enough now to share with you, that it can be done. I did it like Ol' Blue eyes, Frank Sinatra's song popularized in 1968: "Yes, the record will show that I took the blows, but I did it My way." That sums it up.

After that exciting year in the Caribbean, I finally got tired of poverty, heat, humidity, mosquitos and Puerto Ricans, who have severe self- identity issues. I was, for the most part, bored, and Meesna was right, I was not going anywhere. It was time to change.

One evening, I came home after a long day of flying, had a candlelight dinner with Lynn and announced that I had just quit my job. I said that I was thinking about going to Hyderabad for a while to see family and check out the family hotel business. Then I turned to her, kissed her sweetly on the lips and asked, "Hey would you like to come with me to Pakistan and meet my family?" She was dazzled. She embraced me, dancing on a dizzy edge, gave me a long hot wet kiss and said, "Yes of course Dari, yes." I don't make long term plans, impatient? Hell, I don't even buy green bananas. Who knows what tomorrow will bring? I live in the moment, totally. Play it by ear. It was my first trip to Pakistan since I left four years ago. It was 1979.

I choose to look at the brighter side of things. Staying positive. Never give up.

I bought us two round-the-world tickets. Lynn and I flew to Hyderabad after a grueling 18 hours flight in a tightly packed Boing 747. My family welcomed us, but we couldn't sleep together, despite our protests. Sleep in separate rooms. My girlfriend had her nose pierced by one of my sisters. Lynn was a very gracious guest; she was sociable and easy going. She mingled with my sweet sisters and showed them how to exercise at home. My sisters, like most local women, lived sedentary lifestyles.

Females did not exercise as there were no gyms or spas in Hyderabad. Women were supposed to stay home, baking cookies and preparing meals for the male members of the family. They generally did not come out in the streets unescorted.

My parents insisted on a wedding party, so we threw a bash, inviting about 200 people. Ironically my present and lawfully wedded ex-wife attended the ceremony, sitting right behind Lynne. I noticed her stealing looks at me and chatting with my American girlfriend, cracking jokes and having a jolly good time, not knowing that she would become my bride a few years later. I didn't know it either.

I was completely assimilated into the West and proud to call it my chosen home. I think I was the happiest, most joyful man in search of good to do, and I carried no grudge, anger or bitterness toward anyone or anything. This would be my mantra until 2006. Next quarter of a century would be a live well lived, happy and adventurous.

I believed that the best had yet to come and it sure was.

8

CRIMINAL LIFE

WHILE we were in Lahore, Lynn and I got caught up in the 1979 Anti- American riots. The U.S Consulate had been set on fire by an angry mob made up of hundreds of rioters. A few rioters threatened to hurt my 'white girl.' **I took a few of them down.** Luckily, some good men in the crowd came to our rescue, averting a near disaster. Those good men escorted us out of the crowd to safety. The mob was out of control. Rioters were chomping at the bit to hurt the American girl. Gang rape? Lynn is lucky to be alive today. If it wasn't for those complete strangers, the good samaritans, bad shit could have happened.

Disenchanted with the ol' motherland, the trip reassured me that Pakistan was not for me. Now it is not even pleasant to visit, let alone live. I was too Americanized, too westernized to live in the East, thankfully.

Lynn and I flew to Rome so that Lynn could visit Vatican City and get a glimpse of the Pope. I was along for the ride, looking for opportunities in Europe, sightseeing, and searching. We flew to Sicily for few days (looking for the 'Godfather,' Don Corleone,) and then we flew to Malta, a Catholic Island nation below Sicily. Few former PAF pilots I knew worked for Air Malta. They tried to get me a job with that airline, but in vain. Malta sucked, anyway.

Lynn suggested that, since she had met my parents, maybe I should visit her parents and look for a flying job in Michigan. We flew to Ann Arbor, Michigan, and stayed with her traditional Midwestern parents for a month or more. There were no flying jobs there. Lynn's family was gracious. They welcomed me, and I got along with her father and sisters famously. Her mother and few relatives regarded me with suspicion. I was restless, tenacious, argumentative in a cerebral way, but I had a fun time with her family, and we spent a merry snowy Christmas with them.

I briefly flew for an air taxi service in Youngstown, Ohio. We transported auto parts in a Beech 18, a twin engine, tail wheel historic artifact. Shitty job flying poorly maintained airplanes at night in rough weather, in a blinding snow and with paltry pay. It didn't take me very long to quit.

Khomeini's radical Iranian crisis had just begun. A group of Irani students had taken 52 Americans hostage in Tehran, triggering a 444-day period of captivity. Americans were enraged but helpless, and justifiably. Anti-Brown sentiment was running high in the country, especially in middleAmerica, which along with being called the food basket of America, also provides its sons and daughters to the military. Many tough Midwestern boys wanted to kick my ass, mistaking me for an Irani. The gangster in me would never back down, getting into a few confrontations. In one scuffle later in L.A., I bloodied a redneck, making Lynn very angry with me.

I tried to get a job flying with several major airlines, but they wouldn't hire me. Pilots had a hard time getting jobs back then, plus I was no catch. Looking back, I am grateful not to be hired by any Airline. I consider an Airline career, a poor choice- redundant, long hours sitting in the air, bad health, suffering from hemorrhoids, away from family and all that for average wages.

I was looking for the Big Score. I wanted to be Escobar, the dead Colombian Kingpin or at least just fly for him. Had to start somewhere. I was a degenerate looking for trouble. I had heard about some daredevil pilots with a death wish, who illegally flew electronics into Mexico. Electronics smuggling was a flourishing business along the Rio Grande border, from Brownsville to Laredo, Texas. It was illegal in Mexico because the smugglers circumvented huge Mexican import taxes on electronics. The U.S. authorities looked the other way to help out American exports.

I was bored and broke. I bought a used Toyota Tercel in Detroit with my life savings—about $3,000—and headed south, alone, leaving Lynn behind with her family. I promised to call her once I got settled. She tearfully agreed. We had become a loving unit.

In those days, hitchhiking was common. Somewhere along the route, I picked up a hip young couple, students who were going home to Louisiana. I had an interesting experience with them, first in a motel room in Arkansas and later in Baton Rouge, Louisiana. They were grateful for the hospitality and wanted to return the favor. They invited me to stay overnight with them as it was getting late and we were all tired. The young couple had only one big bed in their tiny apartment, and damn, It would be an experience I shall never forget. They took me to heights of sexual ecstasy that I had never known before. She was delicious, and the 'Ragin Cajun' fellow was ... very interesting. Best threesome I ever had, and I have had a few.

My good luck ended in Louisiana, and bad luck started in Brownsville, Texas, a real shit hole on the Mexican border. I got a job with an air taxi service in Harlingen, flying cargo in a Cessna 402. Us pilots who flew for this Airline rented a house in nearby San Benito.

The company had a contract with an airline to deliver packages to Laredo and San Antonio. Soon after I took off, I would put the Cessna on autopilot and rummage through the cargo in midair before the packages reached their destinations. The loot was no chump change, but insufficient.. On this one trip, I found $10,000 cash in a package. Another time, I found a gold Rolex wristwatch. Small potatoes, I was marking time, looking for the Big Score.

Soon I found a mini Mexican cartel in Brownsville and flew as their pilot. The owner of this operation was an ex-con, Bobby, a parolee who owned few airplanes. These smugglers were shoddy novices, and I knew that it was a matter of time before they got busted. We smuggled electronic equipment into Mexico in a Beech 18, an Aero Commander 500 and a Cessna 206. Instinct told me that the DEA had to be watching a parolee with a Mexican homely wife, who owned many airplanes. Crooks always erroneously think they are smarter than the lawmen. 99 percent prison population thinks they were not at fault. Imagine that.

On this one trip that would get me in trouble later, I was in the Cessna 206, flying deep into the mountainous region near Vera Cruz on the Gulf of Mexico. I had previously pinpointed a place to land on my aerial map.

A day or two earlier, I had flown to Vera Cruz on a Mexican airliner and met with my contacts. They took me to a place where I would land. Once we reached our destination, I asked my non-English speaking amigos, who spoke English better than I spoke Spanish, ¿Donde estas de pista?" That was the best I could do in Spanish asking where is the runway. They happily pointed at miles of wide grassy field where cows freely roamed. Fuck me.

After sizing up fields, I chose a spot where I could land. I drove their Ram pickup, up and down the field several times at high speeds, simulating a takeoff in the Cessna 206. Finally, I settled for a particular area and gingerly agreed, "Okay." They were ecstatic; they high-fived each other and to celebrate, took me to several sleazy homes and lined up poor Mexican girls for me to choose from. Language was an issue, but then who needs communication in bed. We had to shop for hours to find the right chikita and a condom. I memorized the landing strip on my mental map.

The following morning, after saddling up I flew a cargo of electronics to Vera Cruz. I landed at the 'marked airstrip' barely keeping the 206 steady. The elated and 'high' amigos emptied the airplane, refueled the tanks from their fuel drums, and while I ate my spicy burrito, they loaded the marijuana bales into the airplane. There were dozens of marijuana bales tightly packed in the cabin. I had ganja bales coming out of my ass. Some of those bales were rammed next to me in the copilot position. The aircraft reeked from the aroma of about 1,500 pounds of shitty Mexican marijuana.

It was time to go. I started the overloaded aircraft and slowly ran it up and down to takeoff speed—55 to 60 miles per hour. Once I had a half-ass comfy feeling, I went back to the take-off point. I slowly opened the throttle and started the taxi and made an executive decision, albeit a bad one, to go. After a rough and bumpy taxi, 206 lumbered forward uneasily. The 206 was ready to be airborne. I gently eased back on the yoke after trimming it back and let the 206 come off on its own. I raised the nose of the 206, and voila, I was in the air. Whew, a huge relief.

Earlier, the Mexicans had laughingly told me about another pilot who did a premature takeoff in a Piper six, with full fuel and planeload of pot. He crashed right after takeoff, aircraft burned to ashes with the cargo and pilot in it. That was hardly comforting. Chihuahua!

Once safely airborne, I flew at sea level, right on the deck (very close to sea level), over the water on the Gulf of Mexico. I did that to avoid radar detection, plus it was more exciting. Flying high gets boring after a while. Speed at height is almost irrelevant, as there is no relative motion, only air speed indicator. Five hours later, I crossed the Texas border with my load and found the abandoned rocky road where I was supposed to land. Sun had already set.

Previously, we had gone driving, searching for a suitable road with scarce traffic near San Benito. I memorized the location of the road and memorized it. Once overhead, I circled around the area, looking for van headlights flashing on and off in the dark, signaling me that I was at the rendezvous point. I landed without my landing lights. Somewhat scary, but exciting. I was happy and relieved to see my cohorts waiting for me. Getting caught in Texas was not a good idea.

Texas was very tough on drug crimes. The State had no sense of humor; it had mandated tough sentences for drug smugglers. The 206 loves short fields, and daredevil me loved landing that baby artfully, like a connoisseur of perfect landings. I was in it for the money, but the adrenalin rush was incredible. Pushing the Cessna 206 beyond its envelope was fascinating.

I landed on the darkened road. My help emptied the cargo, sprayed air freshener and thoroughly vacuumed the 206 for seeds. I took off, landed at Brownsville, cleared Customs as usual and drove home. That trip would come back to haunt me.

On another trip, I flew Bobby's twin engine tail wheel Beechcraft 18 south to deliver electronics to a makeshift airstrip near Oaxaca. Unbeknown to us, bad weather was moving in from the Gulf of Mexico, and the mountains were covered with clouds. I couldn't find the damn landing strip through the sheets of dark clouds. I had no radio contact with anyone, and I was not supposed to be in Mexican airspace. Deep kaka ahead.

We had no such thing as a GPS then; drug pilots simply followed the aerial map. I did not have enough fuel to make it back to Brownsville as the plan was to land in the field, deliver the merchandise, refuel and fly back with the bales. After desperately circling the area, trying to find a hole to break through the thick cloud cover, I was running out of fuel, time, and sunshine.

Suddenly, it dawned on me that I was going to prison. I imagined that I would be caught with an airplane load of contraband in Mexico. I knew of a few pilots who had gone south and never returned or had come back with bullet holes in their fuselages— shot up by the Federales or rival gang members. Holy fuck, I was in trouble. I abandoned my mission and started heading back to the good old USA knowing well that I did not have enough fuel to make it back to Brownsville. Horror struck. I was going down. With a planeload of illegal electronics, I could not land at any airport to refuel. No papers. I imagined getting butt fucked by a big tattooed Mexican in prison.

The storm had moved in; it was raining cats and dogs, with hellacious winds, lightning flashed all around. I was flying at sea level over the Gulf, say, fifty or so feet above the water. I saw the awesome power of the raging water. I was trying to avoid radar detection, Federales, and rival gangs. The old fighter pilot in me, for once, was scared, not knowing when and where the fuel would run out. *Houston, we have a major problemo.*

I cursed myself for not checking the weather forecast before I left. Complacency had set in, and I was becoming careless. Memories of my fighter flying days were getting into my head, making me think I was invincible. So get ready, Mr. Hotshot, I told myself, nature has some punishment in store for your smart ass. I was calm and quiet on the surface, like a duck, but underneath, I was paddling like hell. I just didn't want to be paddling underneath the surface of the Gulf of Mexico.

I kept my eyes peeled for a safe place to land, hating myself for being so fucking stupid. The training for simulated landings during emergencies, drilled into me by PAF, would come in handy soon. I do perform best under pressure.

I didn't have much time; daylight was fading fast. Pouring rain and hail battered the plane, visibility was near zero and lightning continued to flash all around, giving me quick successive glimpses of water and nearby land. I was sweating bullets. Game over baby, I sure as hell was going down. O'God, Jesus, Allah, Swami, whoever, please help. I am not a praying man, but I wished I was at that moment—make believe and get comfort in self-delusion.

73

Isn't that what the faithful do, pray, believe ... and get ... Nada. Do they quit? No sir, fools will double down on the Lord.

North of Tampico, Mexico, approximately 200 miles south of the border the fuel warning light came on and one of the engines started to sputter from fuel starvation. Seconds later it died, and then the second engine died. Complete silence, except the rain, hail and lightening sights and sound. The sweet sound of the noisy twin radial engines was replaced by an eerie silence inside the cockpit. I mustered up all the strength I had and remained calm and focused. Grace under pressure. I pulled up as high as I could, exchanging speed for altitude, which was limited due to the cloud ceiling. I have never been so happy to see the amazing lightning display of nature, making land visible from the air occasionally. Only in the movies, I mused.

Blinding sheets of rain and hail made visibility close to nil. I frantically looked for a suitable place to land. After about a minute of scouring the land, I spotted a barren field that looked semi-suitable for landing. No options left. Having no choice, I glided the Beech 18 down, barely above the stalling speed and made a landing approach to a small patch of farmland. When engines fail, most rookie pilots—read: doctors, executives, weekend flyers—panic and have a tendency to pull up on the nose, losing flying or gliding speed, which is a deadly mistake. Below gliding speed, the aircraft becomes dead weight.

The Beech landed in a half foot of mud and potholes, shuddered violently during the landing roll and came to a stop. Complete silence. I must have sat there in the Cockpit quietly, trembling, listening to the sound of falling rain and hail.

Flying is designed for the birds, not human beings. One is safe with one's feet firmly planted on the ground. The lure and addiction of flying are hard to resist or describe. Once you experience it, you are happily ruined forever. Not all of us have the aptitude to be pilots. Just like not all of us are stoners, gamblers or losers. Either you have it in you or you don't. Best not to push against nature. A crude saying I heard the other day; If it flies, floats or fucks, rent it, don't buy it, schmuck!

I was shellshocked after the 'safe' landing. It's a safe landing, if you walk away alive. I climbed out of the airplane and inspected for damage. The tail wheel had been sheared off. It was completely gone. The main tires were buried in mud. Rest was in one piece. There was no one in sight for miles. Soaking wet I started walking, then running from the scene of the crime. I had to put distance between me and the airplane full of illegal cargo. I ran for miles, slogging through the mud in freezing cold temperatures. I was bombarded by rain, gusty winds, and hail. I didn't know what else to do, so I kept going, developing a severe case of hypothermia. Finally, I made it to a village at dawn.

There were no cell phones then; I used a public phone to call a number that I had been given in case of such emergency. Communicating with my contact was tough. I noticed that two local cops were looking at this disheveled man with interest, and they weren't smiling. My contact, a complete stranger, arrived in a pickup, before the cops could put their slimy hands on me. He whisked me away in time to a safe family house, not too far. I stood in front of the stove, trembling from cold and fear, and thawed out for hours. I still wasn't sure if I was going to Mexican jail or to the United States. No one spoke English. Frustrated and uncertain I fell deep asleep, not knowing what tomorrow held.

The next day, I woke up to smiling Mexicans. After a hurried breakfast, I lead'm on a chase to find the abandoned airplane, taking along a few drums of fuel. Villagers had heard of a plane sputtering the night before. We spotted the Beech 18 sitting in the mud where I had left it. The storm had passed. Apparently we got to it before anyone. We emptied the electronics into pickups and fueled the thirsty plane. I thanked my saviors and instructed them to hold the tail up by grabbing the stabilizer and run with me when I start to roll. They all nodded.

I fired up the engines, did my pre- takeoff checks and gradually moved the throttles up, developing power. The Beech started to dig itself out from the mud and crawl forward slowly. I gradually increased power with the two guys holding the tail up and running with the plane until enough propeller wash (wind) was generated by the engines for elevators to be effective. Soon the plane picked up speed and shuddering violently but lumbering forward, - lo and behold - I was airborne.

The empty aircraft was light and had just enough fuel to make it back to the United States. I flew out of the field, circled the area and saluted my help by flying low with wings waggling- a victory dance. I headed back to the States and landed at Brownsville without any problems. Landing a Beech 18 at the airport without a tail wheel was embarrassing. Customs officials got a good laugh, they had seen worse.

I didn't want to be a drug dealer anymore.

The trip had scared the living shit out of me. I was done. That was the end of my fledging smuggling career. I told Bobbie I was done. We parted ways and I took my part of the profits in pot— about fifty pounds of dirt weed—packed it in black trash bags and kept the stash in the attic of the rental house that I shared with two pilots in San Benito.

While asleep, I heard semi-loud squealing and shrieking noises coming from the attic. I was puzzled. Who could it be? Come to find out, the damn rats had bitten into the trash bags. They were eating the ganja, running around loaded and having a jolly good time. I couldn't believe it. I thought their behavior was strange at first, and then, it was hilarious. They were high, having a rat party!

A couple of days later, I sold the car, loaded the rest of my belongings in trash bags (minus the rat feed) into Bobby's Commander 500 and prepared to get the hell out of Texas. Bobby thought that his airplane was getting too hot and that it was best that I get it out of there and deliver it to his contacts in L.A. I gladly obliged. A friend I met by the name, Goodman, who lived in Alaska, was visiting me to check out the lay of the land.

Before I said goodbye to Brownsville, I took Goodman and few buddies for a joyride in the 206, by the beach on San Padre island.

Flying low n' slow over the water, as we approached the bridge, my buddies started to voice concern, "You are not going under the bridge, are you?" I heard someone say. With adrenaline running high, on a whim, at about 160 miles per hour, I flew a Cessna 206 right under the bridge, a tight fit. Dangerously close, missing the top of the tail and the wing tips by inches. Extreme sport? A miss is as good as a mile. My pals were not amused. Lost couple of 'em forever. One of them said, " You are a fucking time bomb."

The following day Goodman and I took off for L.A. After a long and tense flight, in pouring rain we landed at my old stomping ground, the Santa Monica Airport. We were met by my younger brother, RG, who helped me unload the contraband, putting the bales in his van in plain sight of law enforcement. A daring, but stupid move. I knew I was pushing my luck.

We took my stash to his apartment in Hermosa Beach, and with the help of his homies, we spread the shit on his living room floor, removed all the stems and seeds and packed the pot in baggies to sell. I sold the pot to my old contacts, mostly Blacks and Latinos in South Central. I collected all the money I had made from the sale of contraband. I was moving as far away as I could—to Alaska.

I took the few leftover pounds of ganja, packed all my shit, went to LAX and boarded the jump seat on a Flying Tiger Boeing 747 bound for Tokyo via Anchorage. Flying jump seats was quite common pre 911. Ken, who I had met in PR and who had encouraged me to come to this magical state, met me in Anchorage. He welcomed me to his beautiful world and rented me a room in his two-bedroom condo. We hit it off and Ken would become my lifelong pal.

The year was 1980.

9

ALASKA

I NITIALLY, I worked as a flight instructor at Wilbur's Flight School at Merrill Field. I later became a bush pilot for hire. I had made about fifty-thousand dollars in illegitimate activities. I hid the cash under the proverbial mattress. Not for long, like a fool and his money is easily parted. I rang up my girlfriend, Lynn, and invited her to come to Anchorage to Be with me. Ecstatic, she promptly flew to Alaska to be with her lover.

Boredom soon followed, as it generally does with restless, reckless, clueless and aimless youth. I needed more action. I went looking for trouble. I got involved with some slimy people Lynn introduced. They were in the business of printing counterfeit money. I allowed them to dupe me into a clever scheme that robbed me of whatever I made in drug proceeds.

They had this perfect system for suckers who had dirty money. They claimed they could double or triple your money by superimposing a one hundred dollar bill over a one dollar bill, which they cleaned, wiping off all the print matter on both sides, right in front of your eyes. Now you had two one hundred dollar bills with same serial number. The one dollar bill was now a $100 bill. Wow!

When I saw that Trick, I couldn't believe my eyes. I fell for it. I went to the supermarket and spent both one hundred dollar bills with the same serial number. Bewildered, I raced to my brother's place, breaking a few speed laws. I got my money, $50,000 in cash, and drove back to the hotel, jumping stop lights and signs. I reentered the lion's den, the hotel room, supposedly to double or triple my money. We were sitting down, having drinks, telling jokes and making bad bills when I passed out.

They had slipped a pill into the drink to do the job. Duh! The master had been beaten at his own game. When I woke up, conmen were gone and so was my money. The room was eerily empty. I lost fifty grand that I had made in the drug business. I couldn't report it to the police as they would question the source of the money. I went as far as going to the office of the Secret Service and started to make a report, but then, changed my mind. I turned around and walked right out, leaving two Secret Service agents scratching their heads. I had been had big time. It was unbelievable. That would be the last time I ever allowed myself to be taken.

Broke, I went back to Alaska. I spent that winter, skiing, thinking, reloading, reading, dancing and, of course, partying with regular marijuana use, burning the herb and bonding with fellow burners like Ken and Goodman, who were the connoisseurs. I looked into starting a dating Service, which was still a novelty in those days, but the excitement wasn't enough. Also, I didn't have enough startup cash. Matchmaking comes naturally to me.

I got a job as a pilot with an air charter company at the Anchorage Airport, flying different types of aircraft to rural places. Alaska is the true frontier of incredibly challenging aviation. The terrain is treacherous, with high mountains and unpredictable weather. I was in love with flying and Alaska, totally. I would almost kill myself many times over, doing wild and wonderful, but stupid stunts while flying in the remote parts of this enchanting land of the midnight sun. I was in heaven for a long time—twelve enormously happy years.

Lynn and I had rented a cute little one bedroom cottage in Anchorage, where we played house for two years. We were in love, at least for a while. We went out partying, dancing, playing. She is a good cook and I love to eat..

She knew that the royal road to a man's heart is through his stomach. For the most part, we got along, but at times the relationship became boring. Sex was not as good as it previously had been. The novelty and thrill were gone. I was unfaithful to her and didn't care. I believe that she never strayed and remained faithful, but who knows. Women usually are super secretive about their sexual escapades.

One morning around dawn, I was making love to her, and right at the most critical time, where not only you don't want to pull it out, but instead shove yourself into the pussy, there was a hard knock on the door. We were baffled, who in the hell is that? I quickly put a towel around me and opened the door. Two plain-clothes cops almost pushed me back in the room. One of them pointed to my green car parked in front of our shack, saying, "Is that your car, sir?" Surprised, I said yes that's my vehicle. He said, "There has been a robbery and a killing few hours earlier. The gateway car was described as a green two-door sedan like the one parked in your driveway." They said, "Where was I between the hours of three and four in the morning?" I said right in my bed, snoring in my baby's arms.

They were not amused. One of them politely asked me, "Could you come to downtown with us and consent to an interview and a polygraph." I had nothing to hide. I had not robbed or shot anyone. I promptly agreed. "Could I use the bathroom wash up and change." They looked at each other, agreeing reluctantly, but one of them insisted on coming with me. Fine, come hold my penis while I pee. Now I was being treated like a suspect.

Detectives put us in the back seat of their unmarked car and had one of them drive the green auto to downtown police station. I was not worried but anxious. I had full trust in the judicial system and knew it was a case of mistaken identity. Once in the federal building, they interviewed me for about thirty minutes, then hooked up the wires to my body and I was given a polygraph exam.

We sat waiting for about an hour on pins and needles. Finally, one of them entered the room and said, "You guys can go. Thank you for cooperating with the investigation. You passed the polygraph but could we ask you not to leave the area for next 48 hours until we do our due diligence." Phew, yes sir.

Detectives were earlier driving around and spotted the green car outside our ramshackle cottage. They stepped out and peeked through the door and noticed a tan leather jacket hanging on a chair, similar to the one, the alleged shooter was wearing in the early morning robbery. I always cooperate with the law. Our tax dollars at work.

When I was in Dillingham, hundreds of miles away in western Alaska, working for an air taxi, I got a call from Lynn. She was crying and asked me to come back to Anchorage, Now. She had missed her period. She was pregnant, to my Huge surprise. Holy cow. I did not want to settle down or be a father yet. I had bigger fish to fry. Lynn and I had a long, difficult talk. We reluctantly agreed to an abortion.

I was somewhat insensitive and oblivious to her desire, anxiety and pain. She perhaps wanted to keep the baby. She sadly went through this awful, but necessary, procedure. I believe that to be fair, children deserve two parents and should Only be conceived and brought up by two willing and loving partners.

My favorite playground, Jamaica, is a good example. This island nation is littered with single black mothers. Fathers generally don't give a shit about what seeds they leave behind after fucking without damn condoms. The Rasta culture seems oblivious to it. Result: Many unwanted pregnancies and mentally stunted children raised with irresponsible parenting and absent fathers. I am against females raising children by themselves. A child's rightful needs are ignored by single women seeking motherhood.

Our relationship went downhill after that. I wanted to play around; she did not. We split after a stormy roller coaster ride that took us from L.A. in 1978 to Puerto Rico to Pakistan and then to Alaska. We have stayed in touch, wishing each other well. Lynn is happily married to a friend of mine who has a hairdressing salon. She is a CPA and works for an oil company in Anchorage.

After our split, I continued working at air taxi outfits in the bush. I flew all over this vast, frigid, but magnificently beautiful state for few years.

One of the most fascinating jobs I ever had was flying scientists from the National Oceanic and Atmospheric Administration (NOAA) in a Commander 500 Shrike. I flew the scientists to Barrow, Alaska, above the Arctic Circle. Our mission was to count polar bears and Beluga whales. Yes, they physically count each animal.

My job was to transport the NOAA scientists, flying over the area where they counted the whales. The narrow strait north of Barrow also became the feeding ground for polar bears, who attacked the whales when they came to the surface to breath. Seeing the red blood stains of the Beluga whales on the white snow and the polar bears running around in a feeding frenzy was a *National Geographic* photographer's dream.

We were based at a naval facility at 'the roof of the world,' as Barrow is affectionately known. I must have had half dozen near-death experiences flying in bad weather within sight of polar bears, wolf packs, and other animals. I would venture to say that, in those few years of bush flying in bad weather, those near misses were always my fault.

Most of my life, whenever shit went wrong in my life, I looked in the mirror and there was the culprit, me. Taking responsibility makes it easier to snap out of the doldrums. It is a miracle to be alive. I was daring, but careless, with a devil-may-care attitude. I was probably good at flying, but carefree, even reckless. I should have faced calamity. The law of averages should have caught up. Taking too many chances can't be good. For many people, Murphy's Law has been a reality. Murphy's Law states that anything that can go wrong Will go wrong!

In this decrepit trailer in Anchorage that the air taxi outfit had as an office, I met a cocky Swedish fellow who sold aircraft for a living. In between flights, I used to hang out at his office, which he rented from our landlord. I had made a decision, not to fly for hire; I was sick of being a commercial pilot. Incidentally, I never did fly for hire again. I would fly only private planes from then on.

I watched this plane broker putting a deal together and thought that I could do a better job than him. He was a schmuck, but he was making money. I spoke to my friend Goodman, who reluctantly agreed to go into partnership with me. We both put up $1,500 each and went into business for ourselves. I resigned from my job, telling my Okie boss to shove it where the sun doesn't shine.

Aircraft brokers are almost All white, rural, aging, barely educated and conservative. I was brown, urban, young, educated and liberal. A small difference. I didn't care. I never had a 'poor me' or 'discriminated against' bias, the feeling of reverse racism that many Blacks have in the United States. I thought nothing of it and marched ahead, even saw it as an asset.

I set up an office at the Anchorage Airport, brokering small planes like Cessna, Piper, and Beechcraft. Goodman though kept his job flying DC-6's for a cargo airline. I worked hard to get our new business going, and saw a good potential in it, but

Goodman was not as optimistic at our startup operation. He preferred the security of a job. We mutually agreed to part company as partners, and I bought him out.

I was now the sole owner of Anchorage Aircraft Exchange.

Afghanistan had just been invaded by the Soviet Union, and the United States and Pakistan were working together to defeat Russia's plan to gain access to the Indian Ocean. Pakistan, for a decade to come, would become a linchpin in this political and military quagmire between the two super powers. I wanted a piece of that action and to get involved in some fashion. I thought about joining the American spy agencies and work in the lawless tribal belt of Pakistan. I asked myself, ***Why don't I become an international arms dealer?*** I had no criminal record. No one knew about my shady life, or so I thought. To gain experience and feed the adrenalin, I applied for a job with the DEA in 1981.

Anchorage being a small city, The-powers-that-be knew all the players in town, especially a brown Pakistani-American in the aviation business. After an initial, lengthy and complex correspondence with the feds, I was invited for the final interview at the Federal Building in downtown Anchorage. At least I thought I was going to be a federal agent- albeit a corrupt one. I was walking into the lion's den Again.

Thanks to the information I had provided, government computers had a match. I could be the man, federal marshals were looking for. Unbeknown to me, Jackson County in Texas had a warrant out for my smart ass. Well, I entered the DEA office and the interview began. I was politely questioned about my possible links to illegal activities in Texas in 1979. 'When did I get my ear pierced' I was asked. Two federal marshals appeared from nowhere and cuffed me. Arrested!

I guess that, like most lawbreakers, I had misjudged the power and reach of the law. The Mexican gang of twenty-one smugglers had been busted. Twenty other gang members were either in jail, missing or dead. Their pilot, a Paki with an earring was also among the missing until I walked into the DEA office expecting to become an agent. The irony was that I knew the agents who interviewed and arrested me. They were fellow pilots.

The aviation community was small. I stuck out like a sore thumb.

10

REDEMPTION

S TEPH was a model-like Caucasian girl. She was barely 18, with
whom I was having a steamy hot, coke and alcohol fueled
affair. This twit was fucking my brains out, making all my white
friends jealous. She was very supportive of me and came to see
me for the next two miserable days while I sat in a cold cell awaiting extradition to Brownsville, Texas, the cheapest place to live
in the United States.

My friend, Hal, a big dick lawyer, came to my rescue. Hal and
the DA were pals and flew planes together. Hal and I had done a
few aircraft deals together. He was a resourceful fellow who frequently let me ride his Harley-Davidson. Hal died in an airplane
crash around 2005.

I was arrested on a Friday, which meant that I could not see
the judge and get bailed out until Monday. I didn't want to pay
and told Hal that I lacked the funds for his fee. My good friend
Hal pointed at the Rolex watch I had previously bragged about,
the one that didn't belong to me anyway—the gold Rolex that I
had 'found' midair in Texas. Extortion?

I appeared in front of a federal judge on Monday. Of course, I tried to weasel out of it, claiming they had the wrong man. After all, I was an upstanding member of the community, or so I claimed. The indictment was two years old. As it turned out, even the DA in Jacksonville was ambivalent. On Hal's assurance, the judge in Anchorage, who knew of me, released me on my own recognizance. I had everyone convinced that they had the wrong guy. The DA in Texas offered me the opportunity to take a lie detector test. If I passed, I would be set free. That easy? I could beat the machine. No problem. Surely it would be easy for a habitual liar like me to beat the stupid machine. I went to the local university and hired a tutor to train me to lie on the machine, to fool the system.

The tutor hooked the wires onto my body and had me practice lying for a few weeks. Once I was ready, the DA's office had an independent agency test me. At my expense, a neutral polygraph examiner was flown up from Seattle. The result was disastrous. I failed the test. The system won. I could have killed the college pro who trained me. Not only that, but to add insult to injury, my nymph flame, Steph, dumped me.

Her snooty mom, who was my half-assed friend, convinced her daughter that I was a loafer, a lot older, a loser and a jailbird who was going nowhere, but down. That hit me real hard; I must have been in puppy love. I cried uncontrollably and pled with her not to leave me. I seriously could not sleep or eat well for days. Psychological suffering is said to be worse than any physical pain. The bitch dumps Me? Lord of the Universe.

After I had failed the polygraph, the Alaskan judge ordered me to report to the Texas authorities. I had to fly to Brownsville, hire a lawyer and begin negotiating with the local DA, a redneck Texan, or is that redundant. After some hard negotiations, I accepted a plea deal. I always take responsibility and not hang a sword of Damocles, of guilt or regret over me. I do not regret the past because if I knew better then, I would have done that. I am not a Catholic who is drilled with guilt trips.

While awaiting sentencing, I had time to think about the things I had done in my life that had led me to the brink of incarceration. I seriously thought about running away to Jamaica, Australia or anywhere but Pakistan. I was terrified of going to prison. I love freedom, flying, fresh air, fucking and blue skies. I didn't want to get butt-fucked or be someone's bitch in prison. I can't fathom why people like getting drilled in the ass.

It was time for deep reflection and introspection. I fell to the ground and promised the gods—that I don't believe in—that if I was spared from jail, I would become the best man I could be. Oh, pretty please, gods, help me. I promise solemnly promise, I will make a covenant with you, pinky swear. Redemption?

I was given the choice to either work with the government by going undercover as a snitch or accept the felony plea deal of three years. I took the plea deal as snitching was not very appetizing, duh. I did not want to be a snitch. Do you? I pled guilty to the federal charges of conspiring to import controlled substances. I agreed to a three-year suspended sentence and probation. I received no jail time at all; the gods had won. I would have to remember my covenant. That experience may have been a turning point in my wandering life. I may have had another paradigm shift, like crossing the rubicon. That terrible episode in my life may have been a blessing in disguise.

The system was already punishing me, so why would I want to punish myself anymore? People generally cry over spilled milk—things they have no control over. Should have, could have. Fuck that, not me; I move on and never look back. Snatch the damn rearview mirror of life from its mounting and throw it out the window, rid yourself of the past. I remember the lessons, incorporating them positively in future life design.

Almost everything that happened to me happened impulsively; shit occurred instantly. That was the way it was during most of my youth. I had no major plan, no financial goals, and no self-imposed time restrictions. My central focus was on wanting to be happy, free and prosperous. I would just do my best at any given moment, and hopefully, it would be the right thing to do.

I try and only promise what I can deliver. I remember my promises. I Intend to deliver. I had made a promise to the gods, and I was going to deliver. I had vowed that there would be no limits to my attempts for recovery and pursuit of excellence. But I've got to admit that the reckless in me raises its ugly head everywhere. While I was awaiting sentencing, I was asked not to leave the area. How are they going to find out? I took a flight to Ixtapa, Mexico, and took long walks on the beach and did a month long meditation and reflection while walking, running and jogging on the beach. I don't have to sit in a Buddha-like position in a quiet room with candles 'n shit. What went wrong? How could I correct it and not repeat those mistakes and change the very fiber of my cock, I meant thought. Smiles.

I went back to selling airplanes in Alaska. The Federal Aviation Administration (FAA) did not revoke my pilot's license. I fell through the cracks, as I always have. Ordinarily, if you get a felony flying conviction, the FAA revokes your pilot's license. But I was still bored!

Getting high on pot became my recreational pastime. Pot is insidious in a wonderful way for those whose body chemistry rhymes with it; it creeps up on you and becomes your companion. Many people I know just don't like it. Their body chemistry rejects it, perhaps like I never liked pills or cocaine. Ingesting smoke of any kind has to be bad for you. It contains hundreds of carcinogens. I guess it is both- reconciling risk with reward, reasons why people smoke. But if you have to get intoxicated, then it is better than liquor. I have been burning the herb modestly for over thirty years. I am in reasonably good shape.

I was a serial womanizer, clubbing at night, drinking, smoking, and getting into difficult situations. The FAA suspended my pilot's license briefly for doing aerobatics too close to the ground while buzzing a girlfriend's house on the outskirts of Anchorage.

While living the carefree bachelor life, I had begun to feel a change within me. I began to feel like settling down and growing roots. I guess some sort of paternal instinct had kicked in. I wanted to be a father, yesterday. I wanted to have children, but there was a small problem, and it was obvious. No need to call Houston. I had to get married first.

I felt invincible. I have always had a sunny disposition, capable of doing anything. I have been able to focus like a laser beam on any task that I set my mind on. Mistakes and failures don't scare me as they are part and parcel of the process of life and living.

Goals must be consistent with one's resources and abilities. It is challenging to raise good children in the United States, where divorce is rampant and children are surrounded by all kinds of drugs and other temptations. I wanted to take on the challenge. I also felt that marriage to a Westerner might land me in divorce court as I was not a suitable mate by any standards—track record was poor.

The West accepts divorce as a normal cost of doing business, unlike where I came from. Divorce is a bad word. Pakistani parents are expected to weather and survive marital turbulence and storms. I was no exception. I wanted my future children to have a traditional two-parent family. With that fuzzy, but basic plan in mind, I took out a mortgage on a two-bedroom condo in Anchorage, for $82,000 in 1983. That was my first home purchase. Very empowering, exciting. Lacking credit, I had to collaborate with a crooked real estate agent to qualify. I would be growing roots for sure now. I invited my pal, Ken, to live with me and help pay my mortgage. We got along famously.

I was dating a redheaded chick named Laurie in those days. She had a strange affliction. Her clitoris was covered with a tiny flap of skin, which she said precluded her from having orgasms. Laurie wanted it surgically removed. Ever heard of such shit? And she did it too. She convinced me that I had better go to Pakistan and have an arranged marriage. Laurie was very persuasive, so I decided to go back to Pakistan and look for a wife. Yes, I went wife shopping. I wanted a traditional marriage for the sake of stability and for the safety of my would-be children. What better in life than to be a responsible father?

I gave myself thirty days to find a wife. Yes, thirty days, I told you, I don't fuck around. Upon arrival in Pakistan, my six sisters and countless other family members started looking for a wife for me. My dear, younger sister, Az, helped me find a bride. Az graduated from a medical college, met a wealthy tycoon, married her and never practiced medicine, pissing me off. I wanted her to be a doctor and serve humankind. She is now happily married with several children. We have been very close, growing up.

We interviewed most of her friends but had no success. It was the most important decision of my life, and I was in a damn hurry. I must not have been thinking right. That was obvious. I was also sick with a fever. I get sick when I visit Pakistan without fail. My system has a hard time adjusting to the contaminated food and water. Mosquitos carry malarial sting.

One day, we were at a wedding, where suitable candidates are usually spotted and matched by elders. I saw a lovely girl who looked familiar. She was looking at me out of the corner of her eye, and I couldn't keep my eyes off of her. Az reminded me who she was. She belonged to an influential family in Hyderabad. She was Bobby's sister; he was my best friend, a fellow Gangsta from the late sixties.

Had I seen the mother of my children? The idea intrigued me. I daringly, but romantically, approached her, which is frowned upon in that culture. All eyes were on us with curiosity. I introduced myself to my future Ex and informed her that I was in Pakistan, wife shopping and that I would be interested in talking to her about marriage and possibly taking her back to America. I emphasized that I was in a hurry. She giggled excitingly and replied pleasantly in Urdu, "I know who you are. Talk to my parents." That was tacit approval.

Her sister Nina was her chaperone standing next to her, looking away, but with ears turned toward us. Nina asked me to speak with her elders through my elders. That was the tradition. Being short on time, I had no patience to go through customs and traditions. I knocked on the door to the family home the following day and asked the servants to speak with her father, a patriarchal, intimidating and towering figure. He was a legendary police officer in Sindh. I was invited to the living room; a good sign.

Mr. Khan was a proud man and when I told him about my proposal, he seemed quite amused by my novel and chivalrous approach. He knew our prominent family. Mr. Khan asked me how much money I made. I gave him an inflated dollar number. He looked at my torn jeans with tears and patches and asked me as to why would I be wearing an old jeans with patches, if I had money. I told him that it was considered fashionable, cool in America. He shook his head, unimpressed and asked me not to wear it around them. He had met his match. We would have a turbulent future relationship.

It would be a bitter battle to persuade her old man to consent to my proposal. I continued to woo her. I formalized my intentions by sending my older sisters to see her parents. My parents wouldn't go because they had been turned down before. Apparently, they had done this sojourn twice before. They were politely turned down.

My would-be wife would tell me later that she had wanted to be with me ever since we were young that she had a crush on me growing up. She leaned on her parents to make it happen.

Her stern father was opposed to my proposal because I was too liberal and too Western or American and I drank, I fucked, smoked and partied. He had raised his daughters traditionally in the Eastern ways, and, therefore, it wouldn't be a good match. In hindsight, the old man was damn right, as events would prove in the following thirty years of our ill-suited partnership. We were like oil and water, but opposites attract; that is a magnetic reality.

My family, too, was opposed to the marriage as they also thought we were mismatched. I relentlessly and doggedly pursued her and didn't take No for an answer. I secretly courted her, on the telephone and in letters. I used to write notes to myself about my beliefs, principles, values and so on. I made copies and federal expressed them to her so that she could get to know whom she was marrying. I wanted to reveal myself to the mother of my future children. She was certain and needed no assurances. I doubt if she ever read my notes to myself, perhaps just a cursory look. Reading bores her to my chagrin.

I flew to London and enlisted help from Bobby and from her eldest sister, Peena, who had earlier migrated to UK. Her father finally, but reluctantly, agreed, warning her rebel daughter that she was making a blunder and that she was nuts to want to marry me. He even hired an agency in Alaska to check up on me. The response was negative, confirming the fears of our elders, which we disregarded. I even contacted Baba Saeen, in Hala and requested him to talk to Mr. Khan. Little influence peddling has its benefits; its who you know, especially in Pakistan.

A year or so later, on December 24, 1983 we were married, with pomp and pageantry. Simple and frugal man that I am, I opposed an elaborate celebration but was quickly overruled. We had a large traditional wedding, with 1,200 people or so, paid for by the in-laws. Several goats were slaughtered to feed the guests who came with their entire brood and were always hungry. I refused the traditional dowry. All I wanted was a wife to bear me children, not money and not love, which I thought that we, as partners, would make and cultivate.

Baba Saeen was my best man at the wedding. He sat next to me and whispered in my ear, "Son, we have heard that you Americans take this matter of marriage as child's play, frequently ending up in divorce." His voice turned somber and commanding. "I have given assurance to Khan Sahib that Allah willing you would not do that. Now you have to give me your word that you will not let me down and muddy the family name, ever, by divorcing." I promised him that I would not take this matter lightly. I was serious!

That night I made love to a very shy, sexy, 28 years young virgin woman. She left her home and moved in with us in my parent's house. I was ecstatic. Shortly thereafter, I came back to Alaska, leaving her behind with my family as tradition went.

A few months after our formal wedding, my bride left her country, her world to come to the United States to join me in Anchorage. She knew no one in Alaska. We did not know each other, nor had we formally dated, except for a few times when she came and stayed with her sister Naz who lives in Austin, Texas. Naz played a critical role as her confidant, facilitating our union.

My sister-in-law Naz is a lovely woman with two adult children, a boy and a girl. They all were to become an integral part of our family. Naz's daughter, MJ, would become my third daughter and a lovely friend for years to come. Her brother, Alee, is a beautiful man, eccentric, but in delightful ways. Both of them would become my lifelong friends, my other children.

The very first week of my bride's arrival, I realized that we had made a terrible mistake. Quarrels and disagreements started right away with us getting into serious conflicts. I wanted to divorce, she refused and dug her heals saying we will make it work that she will change. Divorce is not an option, she declared. Call me naive, ignorant or innocent, I thought, yes perhaps people can change. Just cause I can, I assumed she could, anyone could. Years later I would discover that, no, people don't change. Though there are few exceptions to the rule. Dye gets set early and cements over years.

The next thirty plus years will prove that her old man was right. We could not cultivate love or even cohabit as civil housemates. Brief periods of good times will be punctuated by long periods of silent anger and resentment. Irreconcilable differences. The war of the Roses will be an understatement.

For the sake of children and other reasons, we would stay together- mostly unhappily. I am not going to sit here and not take responsibility. We were just chemically mismatched. She is a conservative and traditional woman, married to her customs, and you know me by now, I was a wild man, liberal, unpredictable.

I went to work, hard and smart, and sold hundreds of small airplanes to hunters, fishermen, trappers, Eskimos, lawyers, doctors, law enforcement personnel, you name it. I sold airplanes to anyone, who could afford it. I dealt in airplanes from single seaters to ten seaters, from as little as $10,000 to $1M.

I stayed out of trouble—which is against my nature—making, remaking and reinventing myself into the best I could be. It was my chance to prove that I could Change. I read self-help and how-to books, and I read biographies of successful people so that I could emulate them. Albert Einstein, Bertrand Russell, Machiavelli, Nietzsche, Dale Carnegie, Socrates and few other deep thinkers were some of the giants who left indelible impressions on me. I developed a burning desire to excel, to change the very fabric of my thought, for the better.

I spent the better part of the 1980s pursuing academic interests, studying philosophy, psychology, anthropology, religion, and theology. I would not forget the covenant I had made with the gods, vowing that I would become the best man I know. I intended to follow through on my word in return for being saved from prison. I keep my promises.

My important goal was not only to succeed in my business and personal life but chiefly to be happy. Now, how do you know if you are happy? What would be the yardstick, the metric? There are no definitive guidelines. Books on self-help, true joy and happiness cram the shelves of bookstores and cyberspace. Each to their own, I would develop a path for myself-recipes, which if followed, would generally lead to peace and happiness.

For me, you are happy if you discharge your responsibilities well and dance and often laugh and you look and feel good. That you respect yourself and others and you have earned the respect of thoughtful people and the affection of children, then I would begin to say that you are perhaps reasonably happy, only you will know if you are, not others. The trick is to develop enthusiasm, goodwill and passion for things and for people.

It would also be a good indicator of one's happiness if one was in love with another person and had a loving relationship. I have been working at it, perhaps not too diligently as I lack that elusive 'friendship.' But the fat lady hasn't sung yet. It may come, I intend to fall in love, hopefully, it won't be too late. There is a lot of fight left in me.

11

LIFE OF THE MIND

I love intellectual debates and disagreements with a sincere inquiry after truth. I have no desire to 'win' these discussions, nor do I have any intention or wish to demean or denigrate anyone or anything. I may appear to be arrogant or conceited, but that is far from the truth. I would not learn until later in my life that one must always speak the truth, but with a caveat. If the truth harms or hurts someone, then hold your truth and refrain from speaking it. Nothing good will come off of it. You may feel good by blurting out your truth, but I would rather have the goodwill of another than some moral or factual victory.

Although my lack of tact, choice of words or manner of speech has offended many, it has also benefited countless others. My two children are my favorite fans. I love to challenge and be challenged. Let the sparks fly. I am rather blunt, sincere and straight forward, which, to many, is intimidating and offensive. I relish meaningful discussions and educational sparring with others. I am happy when proven wrong. Think about it: When you are 'Right' you don't learn anything, but when you are 'Wrong' you learn something new. You stand corrected and won't make that mistake and look like a fool again. That to me is a victory.

You want to be well-informed, respected and a good example to others, especially if you are fortunate enough to be a parent.

Raising good children, to me, is the ultimate challenge. Do you want your child to think of you as a yahoo and disrespect you? Respect is earned not asked for. You cannot buy respect anywhere for any money. Respect comes from the heart; it can only be earned by your good conduct and fair treatment of fellow beings, even animals.

Studies show that the number one reason for inmate violence in prison is due to the perception of disrespect from fellow inmates. People crave respect. The innate need for respect, recognition and affection is perhaps the most important emotional need of human beings. The future would give me good marks as I would raise two very sweet, smart and conscientious citizens. I shall come to them shortly.

Now in my mid-thirties, the huge and well stocked Anchorage library, with a magnificent view of the snow-covered mountains, became my second home. I was a familiar sight with two toddlers in tow. Every two weeks, I checked out half a dozen books, non-fiction, self-help and biographies of great thinkers. I wanted to soak up as much information and knowledge as possible. Albert Schweitzer, Bertrand Russell, and the American forebears were of great interest to me.

Books are wonderful companions to those who choose to excel and want to better themselves. They keep you well informed with facts, figures, lessons and historical data. You learn from them and hopefully get influenced by the wisdom, experiences, knowledge and mistakes of others. I always carried a book with me, which, now, is replaced by a tablet, a personal library in your pocket. It's huge!

You can't change others, the only person you may be able to change is you. 'Change' is an interesting phenomenon. It occurs only once in a blue moon. You will be pissing into the wind, trying to change your friend, your adult offspring, your employee, and especially your spouse. The dye gets set after first decade of life. I was in the best company when I was alone. I developed a strong ego, not a big ego.

It is good to have ample time to yourself so that you can think, read, reflect, absorb, adapt and change for the better. I am always on a quest to excel and be the best I can be. I especially paid keen attention to developing skills to acquire and develop integrity and respect for myself, as such precious matters of conduct did not come naturally to me. To some who are raised by enlightened parents, such stuff is as natural as breathing. I had to work hard at it, and it has been a work in progress, a labor of love.

As I grew older, I started to connect the dots and understand the relationship and meaning of cause and effect, karma and nirvana. I started to pay attention to the nature of integrity and morality. I especially delved deep into the inner kingdom of peace, poise and the power of one. I was soaking up information, knowledge, and wisdom at lightening speeds.

I wanted to change the way I did things, my habit patterns, the way I conceived and perceived things. Shit had to be overhauled thoroughly. My inclination to criminality had to be reversed and re-calibrated. I reminded myself about what Einstein had said that the definition of insanity is doing the same thing repeatedly and expecting a different result.

I would check my unbridled ambition and remind myself of what Gautama Buddha said, "The more you have, the more you have to worry about; the less you have, the less you have to worry about." His counsel seems so simple and relevant, yet it is so easily ignored by most people, especially fools and the weak minded, which, unfortunately, are the masses.

I wanted to be the best man who ever walked the earth. I thought, *Why couldn't I be as good or better than fabled, fictional or real historical characters like Christ, Prophet Mohammed, Buddha, Socrates or anyone*? I felt second to no one. Well, at least I can try, it will be a sacred journey. As they say, only God is perfect. It is not in my nature to compare myself to fellow beings. I may righteously feel that, at the very basic cellular and molecular level, I am unique, the result of millions of years of evolution, just like you!

I always felt that I was built for a solo flight, happily marching to the beat of my own drummer, laughing and dancing all the way to the bank ... lol. Bragging? Yes, I'm bragging, but it's not bragging when it is true. I take pride in myself. I try to recognize my weaknesses and work on them. I know most of my weaknesses most of the time, but I take refuge in the fact that I am learning from my mistakes and getting better by the day. Every day is a new day. We all should be getting wiser and calmer as the years go by. Every day can be a beautiful day. I kept trying and succeeding.

Intellectual honesty is hard to come by as it requires strength of character, moral courage and a host of other rare qualities. I always keep in mind that it is not what happens to you that is important, but how you react to what has happened. You are not measured by what you have, what you wear, what you drive, who you bow to or blow. At the end of the day, it all boils down to one thing: Character; how you conduct your life.

If you give respect, you get respect. We are mostly good to ourselves and our loved ones. Even vicious animals take care of their own. What matters is if you are good to others, especially strangers. Being in the aircraft sales biz, I noticed that people reveal their true colors quickly. Money often talks and bullshit walks. I may have developed a giant antenna to spot losers. A dear friend tells me that I should hang a sign 'Bullshit stops here.' Let me share the skills with you, how to spot losers;

Having met so many losers, posers, liars, pretenders, I was beginning to see a common thread that runs through them. Over time, I have developed skills to identify and recognize them. Most people don't think well and go from crises to crises.

I use the word loser loosely. I mean to cover shallow people, impostors, evaders, smoke and mirror con artists, fake, empty shells and suits, insecure, and incompetent wannabes and such.

The chief characteristic of such a person is evasion of truth. Look for signs of deception, lack of candidness, not answering direct and simple questions, hiding behind privacy and properness. Such people have constructed an elaborate structure around them to deceive you into not finding the truth, which may not be as pretty. They are invariably immature, paranoid and wary of exposing themselves as they have much to hide and little to be proud of.

A straightforward and aggressive inquisitor is their worst nightmare. They will avoid him like the plague. They will frown on simple inquiries about themselves. They will take umbrage at anyone prying into their dealings. These are social criminals afraid to be found.

Losers generally live beyond their means around flash and dash. They damn money and spend foolishly to impress others. They won't meet your gaze and instead divert to inconsequent or big, complex issues to baffle you.

Losers surround themselves with people but have no real friends. They always have a plan, a product, a scheme, and some snake oil to get rich, with your money, of course. They will frequently interrupt and manipulate the conversation to gain control. You have to ask a million questions to get a simple straight answer. They would volunteer nothing and resent the intrusion into their lives. They will try to talk in circles and confuse you with their bullshit. They abhor seekers of honesty, frankness and straight talk. They claim to know a lot of people and places, name-droppers. Drugs are often central to their lifestyles.

Losers develop posh manners, designer clothing and slick ways, in order to fool others as most people are easily impressed with symbols and appearances. Losers have not developed enough inner strength yet and suffer from inferiority complex, and want something for nothing. They are predisposed to using you, drawing you into their vortex of deceit, drama, decay and degradation.

You owe to it yourself to learn to spot these harmful people and not let them into your life and become part of their dysfunction. You may lose your hard earned money, reputation or dignity.

12

GOING BACK TO CALI

B Y the late eighties, I was tired of the bitter Alaskan winters
that lasted nine months out of the year. I had always planned
to leave the cold weather and move to a warmer climate. I was
in my mid to late thirties, in the prime of my wandering life. I
felt isolated and intellectually starved. My incredibly smart and
wonderful pal, Boslo, and few others kept me warm and kept
me from feeling totally isolated. They were the lights that bright-
ened the dark days of the Alaskan winters.

Boslo and I challenged each other to be the best we could
be on the squash court and in the financial and personal worlds.
We bet on as to who would become a millionaire first. We knew
that we both would; it came down to who would be first. The
handsome devil beat me to it. Bastard. Smiles! He is an amazing
man. Boslo was instrumental in instilling correct moral and ethical values in twisted me, bringing out the best in me and guiding
me to become a better man. I literally loved him, we spent the
better part of a decade in each other's loving company, skiing,

playing squash, chasing women and discussing Ayn Rand, the author of *Atlas Shrugged*.

He went on to become a successful builder, marry a European woman and raise a family of four. He bought a couple of aircraft that took them to their mountain cabin in the woods on weekends and holidays to hunt, fish and fly.

Boslo thought I was a quitter and that I was deserting him by leaving Alaska. We were in love (not that kind silly, I said it earlier, I don't do men.) I have never met a man who was as strong, as decent or as beautiful as he was and probably is to this day.

Along with my academic and literary interests, my lifelong interest in wine, women and dance continued at a feverish pace, causing continual marital problems, but my loyal wife stayed by my side. By the late 1980s, I had developed intellectual pursuits and felt starved for the company of like-minded people, plus I was cold, burr. I was always trying to thaw out from the perpetual freeze of the long Alaskan winters. Cold is a killer for me, a deal breaker.

In 1991, after twelve wonderful and exciting years, I moved out of Alaska with $400,000 in cash, an uncompromising wife and two sweet daughters who were then four and five. I sold my turnkey sales operation to a lovely friend, LJ, for one dollar with an option to return within six months and buy it back for the same dollar. I was walking away from a lucrative, ongoing operation making oodles of $$$. I didn't care as I was confident that, after some adjustment to life in the 'lower 48' (meaning *real* America,) I would make it.

LJ was a high school principal who was about to retire. A true prince, a wise, principled, cool guy- straight as an arrow, totally opposite of me. I am anything but straight. LJ was as innocent as a newborn, with integrity and good old horse sense. I looked up to him. We spent many mornings discussing current affairs and the life of the mind over a spliff and coffee. I hated to leave his wise company. I knew I wasn't coming back. I had made a few very good friends whose company and counsel I would miss. I was leaving behind Ken whose friendship would continue to enrich my life. He is presently a captain on a Boeing 747.

On a snowy morning, December 1991, we packed our carryon stuff and left Alaska, destination unknown. The moving company would deliver household stuff weeks later to wherever we asked them to, such was our uncertainty-fascinating. I was going to ride that train south till the tracks ran out on the West coast by the sea. The East Coast and the Midwest didn't interest me; the South wasn't even a consideration. My metrics; moderate climate, no insects, access to a big city and ocean view.

Long ago, I desperately wanted out of Pakistan, this time it was Alaska. I bought a new Lexus 400 for $39,000 cash, put it on a boat for an additional $1,000 and flew the family to Seattle on Alaska Airlines. We picked up the car at the Seattle harbor. The plan was to start in Seattle and drive south on Highway 101 until the road ran out. That is one drive that should be on everyone's Bucket List. I was determined to find the place that was most conducive to our needs and wants. Failure was not an option. I would keep driving until we found the best place to work and live on the west coast, a place where our daughters could grow up and not have to go too far away for school.

Talk about their future education. I wondered if one has to be a physicist, doctor, lawyer or high achiever in any field? People put too much emphasis on the importance of degrees. I don't. Some of the most ignorant people I know have multiple degrees while some less educated people I know are wise and well informed. We planned so our daughters would be around, all our lives and be our lifelong friends. Their unflinching love and support would sustain us through thick and thin, keeping us glued together- for better or for worse.

I have a fierce, fiery, love, respect and admiration for both of my daughters. I was full of hope, ambition and sparkling optimism for our future. No fear of failure. We had a good thing to fall back on. Life in Anchorage was not bad at all, in fact, quite good.

We headed south on Highway 101 and drove down the stunningly beautiful coast. The journey began in Western Washington, traveled through Oregon and crossed into northern California. Breathtaking views! Going through the centuries-old redwood forest was a surreal experience. The four of us sang and danced in the white Lexus on our way south during that amazing and memorable ride.

It was December, very cold and foggy, but majestically beautiful. I saw the winding road behind me in my rearview mirror. Instinct told me that I would not be taking it back, and I never have. Once out of a place I keep moving forward, never going back, be it Alaska, Puerto Rico, the UK or Pakistan. Only the lessons and good memories remained. No junk, clutter or stupid shit was allowed in the precious memory compartment.

I found it desirable to cultivate selective memory, as its best to remember the good things and forget the bad, the ugly. I train my mind to do just that. Eject the childhood shit that happens to all of us. Forget the psychological abuse we may have gone through, the sexual abuse by the dad or the uncle, the nightmares, and all that harmful stuff.

You are not a child anymore. Come out of the eleventh century or whenever is it, that you were born. This is 2014, so then let us live in it. Unlearn the dramas you went through. Relearn all that is good. Let's take the responsibility and own ourselves. We do have the power, use it or we may lose it. Let us turn that frown upside down- then kick back and let it rip.

After checking out Seattle, Portland, San Francisco and my old stomping ground, L.A., we settled for San Diego. The weather was critical in my calculations. Fuck cold. We found this incredibly beautiful and affluent seaside community of Carlsbad, thirty miles north of downtown San Diego as the crow flies.

The North County of San Diego is in a class of its own, pleasant, picturesque with a Latin flair. It has one of the world's best climates. Nature has been very kind to Southern California. Earthquakes are overblown; I wondered if the threat of earthquakes exists in the minds of the rest of the Americans, to justify their choices for living in the Midwest, East coast or the worst, the South.

Seeing flowers blooming in the winter, the relatively warm waters of the Pacific Ocean and people smiling, laid back and welcoming, I was sold on California. This was very different from the miserable weather we left behind. I thought I was on another planet. I pinched myself to see if this was really happening. Am I really living in SoCal? Shit, December and flowers blooming and people walking around smiling; Sign me up nigga.

I instinctively knew I had finally come to a place called 'Home.'

I set up an office at Carlsbad Airport with the help of another brilliant friend, Laghee, whom I had met a year earlier at an aircraft auction in Oklahoma City. Laghee, whom we affectionately called 'Godfather,' is a very sweet and smart man who was instrumental in my success in my Californian aviation career. He is a shrewd strategist of the Machiavellian caliber, he taught me many new things. Only after he left in 2005 to run a jet club in New Jersey, did I realize what a wonderful and great friend he was. I miss him now. He couldn't stand living so close to his as he said "evil Ex." Laghee did not like the other sex too much. We remain extremely close and talk regularly.

Two weeks after our arrival, I called LJ in Alaska and told him, I am keeping his dollar bill, he could have my business; I was not coming back. I would rather be a bum on the beach in Cali than the Governor of Alaska. Let Sarah have the job, so she can see Russia from her backyard.

California again, was a dream come true: body surfing, sunshine, dance clubs, sunsets over the ocean, a place of sweet dreams—life in the fast lane. I was in love with life, my work, and the ocean, but above all, I was totally in love with my two little daughters. My girls' welfare would keep me out of trouble, restrained and hedging against my own worst instincts. I felt invincible, on top of the world. The happiest man in the world. I had found nirvana. ***Will this bubble ever burst?*** I would ask.

Life is not supposed to be that wonderful. I was the envy of all who knew me well. I felt that I was the luckiest man on the planet. The year was 1992.

I got a business up and running in short order and started making money. I spent the following many years happily building the business, reading and traveling. Every few years I took my family to Pakistan to visit relatives. My girls hated Hyderabad, guess who must be rubbing off on them. We also went on many cruises. For the most part, I stayed out of trouble. Not for too long. I had this urge (another bucket list item) to fly my own airplane over the Atlantic Ocean and over the Andes to Antarctica.

In 1994, I met a Frenchman, Long, who would become my good friend. Long has a prosthetic leg, the result of a freak mid-air collision over New England in the mid-eighties. He lost his leg, yes, but I tried to cheer him, "Hey man, look at the bright side. You lost your leg but received one million dollars in compensation." He stared at me blankly. I asked myself, would I trade my leg for $1M? No...you?

Long offered me a deal I could not refuse. Long was brokering a plane I could buy in Paris for an attractive price, a twin-engine Cessna 421. I bought an airline ticket and flew to France. I noticed not much had changed in Paris since my last visit in 1975. Long picked me up at Charles de Gaulle airport. Long is very humorous, belly laughs around him.

Paris was disappointing, dirty, dingy, cold, damp, expensive and full of rude Parisians with a large Arab community from North Africa, pulling the collective standards few notches down. To be black and an Arab on top? Life must be awful. I don't understand why some people are Francophiles, people who have positive and excessive good feelings about everything French. I must be a Francophobe then as I don't like the French food, the attitude, the weather and the prices.

Frankly, I don't care about the entire European, Asian and African continents. Only South America interests me. Even in the States, only the western states are my destinations. I will consider Australia, only because my daughter lives there.

I was unhappy in Paris and couldn't wait to get the fuck out of there, but I was also very excited and looked forward to the transatlantic flight. I bought the plane from a pompous Frenchman for $175,000. Banking and other bureaucracy hurdles were archaic. I had a strange thing happen to me before I took off from a small airport on the outskirts of Paris.

I had to go to the bathroom to take a dump. After this fighter pilot had been done dropping a few bombs, I looked for toilet paper. To my horror, there was none. I frantically looked for any suitable substitute to finish the Italian job. Nothing. Panic struck. I reached into my pocket and, very gingerly, took out some large-value francs, the French currency, and used them to unhappily wipe my ass. A very expensive call of nature. That really hurt as I am very thrifty and hate to part with cash unnecessarily, even damn Franks. I felt so shitty, literally and figuratively.

From Paris, I flew to Belfast, Ireland, where I stopped to see my bro-in-law, Bobby, who had settled there years earlier. He was married to an Irish woman and had several children. We spent a rambunctious night drinking beer in a local pub and reminiscing about our college days. Once rested and refueled, I flew nonstop over Scotland and the North Atlantic Sea to Iceland's capital, Reykjavik. I filled up the thirsty fuel tanks, drained my lizard, etc. After resting and recharging, I almost got cold feet. I was having second thoughts about continuing my journey over the water.

I had just flown 800 miles over frigid water. Scared? Hell no, I fired up the engines and took off on a westerly course toward the American continent. I flew another 750 miles and landed in Nuuk, Greenland, the world's largest island. Cold shivers traveled down my spine. It was a stupid idea to make this flight. How the hell did I end up here in the middle of the ocean? I was flying an unfamiliar airplane with unreliable navigational aids and occasional radio contact. Stupid, shit, fuck, suck. Bad idea, but it was too late.

Regulations required that I carried a life raft. Well, how comforting. What the hell would I do with the fucking life raft if I went down? You think I would survive in the middle of the freezing North Atlantic. No, fuck no. I might as well have put the aircraft on autopilot, walked back, opened the door and thrown the damn raft into the ocean.

I flew the Cessna 421 up to 17,000 or 18,000 feet. The distant sight of Newfoundland, Canada, was extremely heartwarming. Yesss, I made it. It was a fucking relief, totally. I may have dodged a bullet.

After that harrowing trip over the Atlantic waters, I thought to myself, *What if the engine had failed?* I surely would be dead. People fly over the Atlantic all the time. Some never make it. I had frozen with fear in the middle of the Atlantic. I will Never be so cavalier ever again. What was I thinking, playing Russian roulette?

I spent the evening with a relative. She lives in Montreal. She looked at that bumble bee of an airplane, I had just flown across the Atlantic, rolled her eyes and slapped me, which was richly deserved. From Montreal, I planned to fly to the States and land in Ann Arbor, Michigan, where I had a potential buyer for my Cessna 421. I was going to make a handsome profit.

I would never make it to Ann Arbor.

The trouble began an hour east of Detroit. As per regulation, I filed a Visual Flight Rules (VFR) flight plan to Detroit, Michigan, the port of entry. By the time I was about a hundred miles out of Detroit, the weather had deteriorated. I was flying through pounding sheet of rain, sleet and lightning with poor visibility. I lost radio contact. I had to fly low due to cloud ceilings that were down to about 1,500 feet. I was lost. The hotshot fighter pilot was not just uncertain of his position, he was Lost.

I landed at the first available small airport, almost overshooting the small runway that was not meant for a twin Cessna. I did not contact Customs. A big no, no. The aircraft had French registration. It was after sunset. It was exhausting after a tiring and nerve-racking flight. I had failed to go to the port of entry to clear Customs and Immigration. Fuck!

After checking into a nearby motel, I passed out. I thought about regulations while having a pancake breakfast at Denny's the following morning. Dumb, dumb, seriously fucking dumb, perhaps reflecting my inherent streak to disregard the law. I cursed my lawless upbringing; I knew trouble was brewing.

After breakfast, I took a taxi to the airport. When I arrived at the airplane, Armed Customs agents swarmed in and their cars blocked the airplane. Customs agents detained me for questioning and had a field day. Perhaps nothing exciting ever happens in that part of the country. Apparently, my buyer in Ann Arbor, Bob Twining, who had been expecting me, got worried when I did not show up and called Customs looking for me.

After a rigorous interrogation, the federal agents confiscated the airplane, suspecting foul play. I objected and got into an argument with the officers. They told me to back off or else I would be arrested for obstructing an official investigation. Airport bums who had gathered, giggled and mocked me. The officers thoroughly searched my bags, the plane and me. They were rightfully suspicious. Who in their right might come flying in over the Atlantic, in a Cessna, without alerting the officials? In their minds, something was wrong. They just couldn't put their finger on it, yet. They confiscated the plane, a little over $10,000 in cash that I had in various currencies—English pounds, French francs, Icelandic krona—and reluctantly let me go, on foot. Bummed, I took a commercial airliner home.

I had to hire a lawyer in Detroit to get out of that mess. Because of my previous record, Customs justifiably suspected illegal activity. A Paki with a record of drug conviction had entered U.S. airspace without notification or clearance while flying a

French-registered twin Cessna purchased with cash. That on the surface looked pretty serious, I would think.

Customs suspected criminal activity. They flew the Cessna 421 to their facility and took the plane apart, looking for any kind of contraband. Customs kept the airplane for about four months while I begged them to release the aircraft. They couldn't believe, I was clean and that failing to get clearance was just an 'oversight' on my part. What was I thinking, dummy.

After some negotiating, I pled guilty to two counts of Customs and Immigration rule violations. I paid a $5,000 fine for each infraction, plus another $5,000 for a lawyer, and my name was put on the Customs watch list. Damn it, how moronic could I be. Sheer reckless and retarded behavior. Bad upbringing kept kicking in. Adopted learning would keep taking a back seat if I didn't watch it, all the time.

Whenever a situation arises, my first instinct is to tackle it swiftly, even inappropriately, especially if it involves money, sex or anything important. Basic disregard of the law was instilled in the fabric of my thought. I have to diligently apply good American-learned behavior to do things correctly and lawfully. It's so hard for a leopard to change its spots, I kept trying.

I traveled all over the world, looking for planes, sex, and fun, especially in South America, as I swore not to go anywhere where it was cold. I had enough snow for this lifetime. I am only going south.

I separated from my wife in 1997. I packed all my belongings into my just bought, Black Lexus and rented a small cottage on the beach in Carlsbad. I hooked up with a yoga instructor, Julia, and fell in love. I was prime and ready. Since I would go only to warmer climates for vacations, I took Julia to Jamaica to play. Traveling together gives each partner a good opportunity to gauge, qualify each other. Of all the places on the water, Jamaica was my best playground - and Havana, the worst. This yogi was such a bitch as a companion; she wouldn't let me fuck her and kept flirting with locals, pissing me off. I hate begging for pussy.

Despite her dramas, we had a great time. I was, by now, used to drama queens, chicks with a sense of entitlement. That was the most memorable trip I ever took, as it was a challenge but also a sensitive and sexual journey into the lover's body and soul. A potential to find lifelong soulmate, if there is such thing called, Soulmate!

I was enjoying the single life to the hilt. The business was doing well, and I was in lust with Julia and in optimum health. I had a routine of working out at L.A Fitness every day before work. I would shit, shampoo, shower, then shave in the steam room, dress up and report to work by eight. I ate well, and I was always happy and in good spirits, going out dancing, regularly. I guess this boy just wanted to play and party. The trouble was that I had an angry family. They felt deserted, even betrayed.

I got to know Julia in the mid-nineties and started pursuing her relentlessly, as I always do when I like someone or something. Initially, we slept together for sex and affection, but later she had me working hard to get laid, like most girlfriends do. I got tired of the pursuit and offered her a deal. Every time she slept with me, I would give her two franklins. I would help her pay her bills. Ok, let's be straight. I was paying her $200 for the privilege of fucking her. Prostitution, hullo. That arrangement worked well for a while. I suddenly realized that I had enough cash, why don't I just pay for sex, Julia or anyone. Julia became the gateway to prostitution.

After a yearlong intense fling with Julia, it was crunch time. She asked me if we should move in together and start a family. "Shit or get off the pot, Romeo," she may have said. "I will feed you well and take care of your brown ass." The temptation was maddening. I loved her yogi meal preps and healthy lifestyle. I was terribly torn between Julia and my family. I have to be honest here. An ordinary man would have caved in. It took all my might to make the painful choice. I was in love, what can I say. Family righteously won. I may have lost relations with my daughters.

Guilt overcame me. I felt that my children, then eleven and thirteen, were distancing themselves from me, the younger one even dissing me. That was unbearable and not acceptable. I wanted to raise good citizens. I remembered my promise, my covenant to my higher self that I would give my girls, full-time supervision, and guidance. Now they felt abandoned, and I thought they could be headed in the wrong direction because of my neglect. It was obvious by their attitudes.

I did not need a shrink or marriage counselor to tell me that I should get back to parenting. The situation gave me an insight into the divorce scene in the West. Oh, how tempting was the 'Other woman.' I almost had my priorities confused, no confusion there. Making the 'sacrifice' was tough but right.

I decided to end the affair and asked my angry wife to take me back. My stern wife came over to my seaside cottage. She took me back, but she made me end my relationship with Julia on the spot, telling me to pick up the phone and call her now. I pled with her to let me do it later, alone, in my own way with kindness, compassion, and grace. She dug in her heels and said that if I wanted to keep the family together and see my children, it was now or never. She knew my soft spot. I wanted to get back with my children. I reluctantly picked up the phone, under duress, and told a shocked Julia that I was breaking up with her. She asked, "Just like that?" I felt terrible. I wished the earth would part under me.

No one deserves getting dumped like that, not even a total bitch. I buckled and sheepishly said, "Yes, just like that." I felt like a douchebag. I had doggedly pursued her for years, and we had an interesting relationship. Bringing a relationship to an ignominious and hurtful end was not my style. I deviated from my own rules and ended my adulterous relationship with the yogi.

I got back together with my wife, but the second honeymoon didn't last very long, and our relationship remained rocky. We were like day and night; we couldn't even agree on the time of day. Ours was a love-hate relationship. During all my difficulties, she had stayed strong, dedicated and kept the family together, but most of all, like Hillary and countless others, she tolerated my peccadillos. She showed resilience, patience and perseverance throughout my wanderings, never strayed and stayed dedicated through my confusion and soul searching. I must have been an asshole, at least in her eyes. I never felt her pain, but instead remained indifferent. Additionally, I had disdain for such 'weakness.'

No matter what, I kept #1 happy and peaceful, keeping in mind the cliché that *it's the journey, not the destination.*

I'm very liberal and open about life, nothing is secret, sensitive or sacred. I am an equal opportunity teller, which has caused me major problems. Have you noticed how people act like everything is a top secret? Their life—Fort Knox—not mine. I would have made a terrible CIA agent. I'm just too damn transparent to a fault—many say—like most people, especially females are rather private. Too private in my opinion. Half the fun of having a secret, mine or yours, is sharing the damn thing with your trusted aides, friends, and family. To me, it's a true joy to brighten our ordinary and sometimes mundane lives with a few tidbits of each other.

Normal lives are often boring, repetitive and lack excitement or novelty. Healthy gossip is good; Gossip that doesn't damage anyone and contains valuable information. It's a window into the hidden and sometimes rotten soul of human beings. Most of us are fallible with flaws and weaknesses that we try to hide unsuccessfully, sweep under the rug. Guess what? We are all like that. Let's get over it. FDR said it was his firm belief that the only thing one has to fear is the fear itself.

I trust in my judgment to trust someone I share a secret with. They will not let me down. In the aircraft business, I would have made numerous errors, had I not shared the specifics of that particular airplane with a few colleagues in the know Before I bought the airplane. By sharing what I was told, I was warned about the pitfalls of the purchase, which they knew about, but I did not, saving me a precious nickel. Even in the personal domain, such gossip can be beneficial to participants. People are too afraid of the unknown. I am not!

13

MR. X

IN the early-nineties, I developed a close friendship with a super-secret, enigmatic, wealthy Mexican businessman. I will call him Mr. X. He was a rather dashing young man in his early thirties. He lived the high life in a posh penthouse overlooking the ocean on Coronado Island, an affluent suburb of San Diego. This exclusive island minutes from the border of Tijuana, Mexico, is home to super rich Mexicans, along with the U.S Navy. The Mexican was the talk of the town in aviation circles. He was the sweetest, humblest, most magical man I would ever meet. He bought and sold jets.

Mr. X was also charismatic, cold and calculating. He was extremely polite, polished and civil. You would never know that this unassuming, short and round man was so talented, so generous, so dangerous. Mr. X was a shrewd visionary with grand schemes and Machiavellian moves. He was almost a genius and believed in his own mind that he meant well and had good intentions. Mr. X totally believed with all sincerity that he never intended to steal money or harm anyone. He doubted that he had ever swindled anyone. A true believer. In fact, he thought, and he made you believe, that he was doing you a great favor by doing business with you.

Mr. X cleverly appealed both to your greedier and nobler motives at the same time and knew that You can be bought. What matters is how much and what is at stake? Well, he had a point there. Almost everyone Is for sale, depends on how much, what's the price and what is at stake. A good case can be made for that argument. Me, being a consummate deal maker—and perhaps greedy like most human beings—willingly and sincerely fawned over him, dealt with him. On many occasions, Mr. X temporarily borrowed money from me at exorbitant interest rates due to his 'Stopgap' cash flow issues.

Mr. X was always in a cash crunch, juggling big deals that frequently involved six zeroes, even several million dollars. Many, many times I may have lent him as much as $100K at an astronomical usury interest rate of $1,000 per day, sometimes for as long as thirty to forty-five days. He generally gave me collateral, a jet, sports car or merely a promissory note. Bastard had my number.

The carrot got bigger and bigger. Mr. X lured me into this or that big deal he was working on and said that he would turn me on to this deal with a huge profit, blah, blah. Keep it a secret, a top secret. He would always pay me back, albeit late, except for the last time. When the interest went over an insane amount, he defaulted. I remember my growing anxiety, the sleepless nights waiting in vain for his calls while he traveled all over the world, piloting his own jets, wheeling and dealing. He kept his deals shrouded in secrecy, causing me to sweat bullets while waiting for the money he owed me. (The big deal he had promised, the big carrot.)

Aviation was a booming business. Everyone around me who dealt with him was making ungodly amounts of money by any standard, thanks to Mr. X. We all competed to curry favor with this mysterious figure. We thought the party would never end.

Was it greed, love, gullibility? I don't know. I was smitten, drunk with both his personal charm and the lure of money.

Mr. X had me and others vying for his attention and the chance to participate in his business deals. We liked him because he made us all lots of money, paid our party bills and took care of the odds and ends, like large restaurant or fuel bills. I started dealing in jets under his tutelage. He was a master of intrigue, a sharp and devious trader and an amazing dealmaker, playing both ends against the middle. The bastard did it with such finesse that you felt like you were in the presence of royalty when you were around him.

He had access to private jets, villas on the Mexican Rivera, five-star treatment in prestigious Vegas casinos and comps in presidential suites. It was so easy to give in to the temptation. He would win and lose hundreds of thousands of dollars. Money was never an object. He carried thousands of dollars in cash in his briefcase. Financially speaking, I learned not to sweat the small stuff from Mr. X. I learned not to be cheap, but to think large and take calculated risks.

I learned to face and fight my own challenges of poverty of spirit, of economic default, of losing it all. Frugal, I watch every dollar that leaves my pocket. I bargain, I dicker and I hurt when I see a large bill for just about anything, whether at Taco bell or buying Geena, a Lexus with cash. Mr. X would routinely tip waitresses a hundred dollar bill. My eyes bugged out when I saw him do that. The Mexican respected me and looked up to me for counsel, many people do. I wish I knew of a 'Dari' who I could look up to, as my consiglieri.

Mr. X and I hung out, traveled, socialized and did business together, enjoying the brighter, finer side of life. He provided booze, fine cuisine, and women. Mr. X hardly ever drank, never got high and was always in control. One day, he talked me into a deal that took me by surprise and one that I could not refuse. He wanted a live show!

Mr. X offered me $2,000 to let him watch me fuck Julia. Yes, two grand just to watch me screw Julia. Being a sick puppy, it interested me. I spoke to my girlfriend about this twisted sexual proposition. After some hesitation, Julia agreed on the condition that she would keep All the money. Well, I wanted a cut (it's in my nature.) She refused. I thought the experience would be erotically unusual, so I agreed.

Mr. X booked us a penthouse suite at the Marriott at San Diego harbor. The room came complete with chocolates, candles, champagne, grapes, golden silk sheets, an ocean view, the whole nine yards. At the appointed time, we met in the hotel lobby, had a few drinks, loosened up and took the elevator up to the top floor. Mr. X pulled up a chair and sat next to the king size bed with a bird's eye view.

Julia and I undressed while he watched our every move. I dimmed the lights, crawled in the bed and let him watch my girlfriend fuck me. Julia was a trooper. She would later tease me, saying that he was probably watching me, not her. It was a sick show without Viagra.

I don't know how porn artists perform for XXX movies, but our live show was an amazing experience. I needed no Fluffer, person hired on pornographic film sets to ensure that male actors are kept aroused. He's the guy who comes in when the director yells 'cut' and the male loses his erection. It's the fluffer's job to get it up, get the actor aroused, generally by sucking his cock. I will leave the rest to your imagination.

My friend made me tens of thousands of dollars, but also brought me major legal troubles, brain damage for which I take full responsibility. I always do as I own myself. I own everything I have and anything I do. I am the governor of my life, my acts and my conduct. Even when I misgovern, I am still the shameless, but the proud, Governor.

In the late 1990s, Mr. X supposedly bought and imported a prop jet, a 1991 Beechcraft King Air C90A, from one of his Mexican contacts. He then sold it to me for a cool one million dollars cash. It was the most expensive aircraft I had ever purchased. When you buy an aircraft from another country, the country of origin—Mexico in this case—notifies the FAA that the plane has been deregistered in their country. International rules then allow the country of import—United States in this case—to register the plane in its database. The FAA accepted the official de-registration from Mexico, thus making the Beechcraft King Air the property of a U.S. citizen, Incredible Me.

I had bought numerous planes from Mr. X in the past. Yes, a few deals were shady, but legal. Maybe some were illegal in Mexico where corruption is rampant. I did my usual diligence as required by law, and paid him the purchase price through an escrow company in Oklahoma City where the FAA is headquartered. Everything was done legal eagle.

A couple of months later, I resold the airplane for a huge profit, over a hundred thousand dollars, to a mega corporation in the state of Idaho. Everyone involved was happy. Let's celebrate and open champagne. Was it too good to be true? Oh yes, just wait until you hear about that major fiasco, that landed me in a world of legal trouble.

I don't care for lawyers (though I have a couple of close lawyer friends) doctors, truckers, ballplayers, pimps, Hummer owners, politicians, fishermen, trappers, hunters; I can go on. Suffice to say that I dislike more than I like.

The buyer of the airplane notified me that the company had tried to resell the plane. That's when they discovered that the former Mexican owner had filed a lien with the FAA, claiming that he had been defrauded by Mr. X, who had not paid him in full. The former owner claimed that Mr. X had paid off some official in the Dirección General de Aeronáutica Civil (DGAC), the Mexican equivalent of the FAA. Fuck me, all hell broke loose.

The Mexican authorities wanted the Beechcraft returned to their country, claiming it was stolen property and that a chick working for the DGAC had been bribed and the de-registration was fraudulent, invalid. The Mexican chick was arrested but what good would that do to me, I was still fucked.

An investigation ensued by the FAA, the FBI and the Department of State. I went into a tizzy and demanded that Mr. X, clear up the lien matter or return my money and take back his damn King Air. He swore that he had fully paid the guy he bought it from. I wanted to believe him, but asked him to verify that he had paid the previous owner.

I had him fly the previous seller from Mexico city to San Diego to meet with us, which he promptly did. An unimpressive, short, pudgy, wet bag showed up. The three of us chatted at Jack's, a popular Del Mar eatery. The meeting was a disaster. It was a Mexican standoff. Neither of them backed off nor convinced me that the other was a thief. A lot of 'he said, she said,' and they could not produce proper documentation for the transaction, which is quite common south of the border or in third world countries. After a complex legal battle, the FAA sided with me, thereby refusing the Mexican claim and setting a precedent for future transactions.

The aircraft became a valid American property, but the FAA documented the incident, thus clouding the title. Holy fuck!

In an unrelated matter, Mr. X was convicted of fraud for forging aircraft records and engaging in other fraudulent activities. Mr. X went to prison for two years. Upon his release, he was handed over to the Mexican Federales and deported. Mr. X is out of the United States, perhaps forever. The three letter agencies (FBI, FAA, IRS) came to my office and interviewed me, scaring the daylights out of me. They were doing their due diligence, making sure I was not involved in anything other than my routine dealings with him. I told them what I knew. I did not know frankly. He wouldn't even tell his left hand, what the right hand was he doing, the man is so secretive. The agents left and that was that.

The IRS was particularly interested in an account I kept in my brother's name with me as a signatory. Why did I have $55,000 in an account outside my regular company books? I told the truth: It was play money that I did not want my wife to know about. The agent smiled wistfully, and that was the end of that.

My younger daughter Geena and I flew Mr. X to Barstow Federal Petitionary in Nevada to do time. While landing on a tight dirt strip in the prison's backyard, I almost lost control of my Cessna Skylane due to the short non-paved runway, rusty approach, and my shoddy landing plan. I lost a friend who made me big money, but also caused me brain damage and legal troubles.

In 2001, the Idaho firm that bought the plane sued me in federal court and won a default judgment of one million plus dollars. I did not have adequate representation in court as I thought it would be very expensive to hire lawyers, and I have a proclivity to shun lawyers. In an attempt to avert a legal disaster, I filed for bankruptcy but pulled back on the legal advice of my bad lawyer, me! Abraham Lincoln had it right "He who represents himself has a fool for a client."

A year earlier, I had made a mutual agreement with my wife to dissolve our marriage. The timing couldn't have been better as I killed two birds with one stone, so to speak. I obtained a divorce and made the default judgment uncollectible. I didn't have much money left anyway, I swear. After the divorce, I moved out as I was single again. Party time!

I never saw Mr. X again. He left many of us holding the bag, the empty money bag. The vultures were circling overhead to get a piece of the carcass. There were many wounded soldiers in his wake, bleeding, strewn along the path to wealth. However, I loved the man. Now Mr. X lives a stressful life in Mexico City where he is facing more legal issues, while licking his wounds. He is rumored to have stashed over ten million dollars before he went to prison. He can never come back to the States, at least legally.

Just recently, his name resurfaced again. He is allegedly involved in a complex conspiracy to help smuggle Saad Gaddafi and his family out of Libya and settle them under fictitious names in Puerto Vallarta, a resort area in Mexico. According to the *National Post*, a Canadian newspaper, who is tracking his moves, he was under arrest for a week or two, then released and rearrested. The Gaddafi incident has become a political scandal, and Mr. X seems to be in a ton of trouble. The investigation is ongoing, with several people already in jail. Mr. X may be in a jam again.

Mr. X continues to live on the edge, defying all odds and evading authorities on both sides of the Rio Grande, the river that separates the United States from Mexico. I wish him well as I have fond memories of our friendship, despite the legal troubles. I do not hold him responsible for any of it. I am a big boy, and I willingly, and with great pleasure, dealt with him, and I'd do it again in a New York second if given the chance. Such is my loyalty, stupidity, love and goodwill for this amazingly beautiful man.

Furthermore, I rarely regret much or hold a grudge against anyone or anything, most of all against myself, as that was my best shot at the time. If I had known any better then, I would have done it. So then why regret?

Regret or guilt is self-defeating, counterproductive to one's health and unhelpful for future growth. Taking full responsibility for one's actions is always a good first step. Life will be lot more pleasant if you look in the mirror First, to see if you see the culprit. It's very easy to point a finger at others and conveniently blame others for our troubles. When you point a finger at others, you forget that other fingers are pointing at you.

Mr. X, now fifty plus years old and suffering from high blood pressure and other ailments, is in the news again, right on the heels of the Gaddafi scandal. Got to give it to the man.

On 9 December 2012, Jenni Rivera, an American singer who is hugely popular in Latin America, especially among narco-traffickers, died in a fiery crash of a Learjet in Monterrey, Mexico. The plane was registered to a shell company, Starwood Management, owned and operated by my good friend Mr. X.

The 1970s vintage Lear 25 took off from Monterey before sunrise and, after twenty minutes in the air, nosedived from twenty-eight thousand feet and plunged to the earth, taking Jenni and four of her band members to a grisly death. The wreckage was scattered over an area the length of three football fields. A seventy-eight-year-old Mexican pilot was at the controls, along with an allegedly twenty-year-old inexperienced copilot. The FAA is investigating the crash as the jet is registered to an American entity.

Mr. X is rumored to owe millions of dollars to the IRS and others. Mr. X also is said to be under investigation by the DEA, suspected of selling jets to the Arellano brothers, the vicious drug cartel from Tijuana. In the mid-nineties, he was indicted for selling a jet Commander to a drug kingpin in Miami and not reporting the cash transaction to U.S. authorities. He was convicted and served six months in prison.

Mr. X just gave an interview to the *Los Angeles Times*, claiming innocence. He said the DEA and others are just jealous because he is a successful businessman in the lucrative aviation industry. He denied any complicity in drug trafficking. He admitted only to selling aircraft to anyone who has the greens. He has a point, but U.S. laws mandate reporting, if suspected criminal activity is spotted. If someone gives you, say, $250,000 cash to buy a jet. The buyer is probably breaking few laws. Why cash? America does business by wire transfers.

A grand jury investigation supposedly has ensued on both sides of the border. He recently texted me, saying that he has money now, but no peace. He has become a slave. Well, once you are beholden to anybody, the government, the Mafia, anyone to whom you owe money or the ones who keep your dark secrets, they will have a sword of Damocles hanging over your head.

I never knew the actual extent of his holdings. He reportedly has an eye-popping thirty-plus jets registered to shell companies that he owns or controls. The planes are worth tens of millions of dollars. The planes belong to 'unnamed' sources that would rather stay anonymous. The man never ceases to amaze me. Imagine the incredible pressure he is under right now. Unbelievable, but true.

I remind myself of the recipes of life that have served me well to this day. To live a simple life, restrain your desires, impose self-discipline and harness your energies. Don't get greedy or excessively ambitious. I cannot emphasize more that having too much money or fame is counterproductive to human health. I struggle not to become a slave of my possessions or passions as they could own me. It's very lonely at the top. I remember staking out my future early in life and telling myself that my life plan should be such that I would not miss out on the finer things in life—sunsets, children, time alone, friends, pussy, just to name a few.

The lure of Big money—millions of dollars—will be too much to handle. Once you go down that path, assuming you have the capacity and ambition to achieve your goal, you can be sure that it will be very hard to do. You will constantly be working. You may miss out on seeing your children grow up or miss forging close friendships as you most certainly will be devoted, almost married, to your work while building your economic empire.

By all means, we should have a strong work ethic, but personally, I learnt to keep my ambition in check as it is very intoxicating. No one goes to their grave wishing they had worked longer and harder; instead, they probably wish that they had loved more or taken more pleasure in the simpler things of life. To stop and smell the roses.

After 9/11, the business took a nose dive, plunging to the lowest level I have seen in my 35 years in the aviation business. General aviation took a big hit. Nobody was flying or buying an aircraft. United States airspace was empty. Being brown, in aviation and given my past record, I was heavily scrutinized by the authorities.

Anti-brown sentiment was sweeping the country. I was heartened by the support of my peers. Even strangers walked up to me and offered their unsolicited support. I never felt singled out because I was from over there. I feel, exude, breathe, love America. I might add that I did work hard to earn this great distinction to call myself an American.

My older daughter, Sheila, then in high school, was addressed by a racial slur uttered by a high school bully who was then jumped on, by all her Caucasian friends. The incident made me weep with pride and joy for my adopted country. Come to think of it, most of us brown people and other legal immigrants have worked hard for our citizenship. We have had to pass several markers and take an oath of allegiance, and gladly I may add, while native-born don't have to lift a finger to acquire one of the most coveted gifts an individual could have: the right to be a citizen of the greatest, mightiest and most beautiful country in the world. I truly was, and always have been, proud to be a Pakistani-American.

Like the rest of us, I was swept up by patriotic sentiment after that horrific attack on New York City. I wanted to get those sons of bitches. Regardless of my opposition to the invasion of Afghanistan or my political leanings, like President Bush, I was ready to attack, invade, nuke, napalm. Just give me a name, a country, a nation, a damn hemisphere, who did it?

World support brought tears to my eyes. South America, Australia, Africa, Canada, India, Europe, even Russia were one with America. The tepid support from Asia was disheartening. What really pissed me off was the disgraceful cheering in most of the Arab world, especially in my own native, Pakistan.

The lull in the marketplace continued for a while. I was bored by aviation and wanted to do something else. I noticed that everyone and their dog was making money in the stock market. I was sharp, good with numbers and street smarts, so why couldn't I do that? But first I applied for an analyst position with our State department. I filled out an application on the internet. The Government, disappointingly, never got back with me.

Why couldn't I make money in the stock market? It seemed easy. I taught myself by searching how-to advice online and by watching Bloomberg TV. I was about to make a move that would cost me half a million dollars (Not Rupees). I sold all my planes and counted my pennies; they added up to a little over a million dollars.

I bought an inexpensive computer for $750, my first ever. I was about to make a devastating mistake. I taught myself how to operate the PC and ... voilà. Within a week or so, I became a day trader. That was another huge miscalculation, a byproduct of my inflated ego? The losses would be gigantic, jarring my confidence.

I woke up in the wee hours of the morning when the markets opened. I learned how to figure out the stock market by watching TV and surfing the Internet. Within three months, the market started to gyrate, swinging in all directions, wiping billions of dollars from individual portfolios, including $500,000 of my hard-earned money. The stock market crashed, bruising not only my bank balance, but also my self-confidence. Not only I lost half a million dollars, I also lost my mind, my compass and my anchor, Me!

The loss battered me both financially and emotionally. How could this happen to me, Mr. Know It All. I thought I already had been there, done that. Not quite.

I learned a valuable lesson: One should stick to what one knows, what one is qualified and trained to do. There is no easy transference of professional knowledge, trained skill and experience, which only time, track record, and results can prove. Proof is in the pudding. After that disastrous foray, I went back to what I knew best, buying 'n selling small aircraft. I even stopped burning the herb so I could focus and not get 'Stupid.'

Life at home sucked. My extracurricular activities and other legal issues led to a parting of the ways with my Ex, physically too this time. We made an amicable arrangement. I moved out, renting a luxury apartment on Moonlight Beach, and left the mansion to her ... Smiles. Had to, you know, the women get batty about real estate. What happens to these 'nice' ladies, when it comes to houses (money?) They turn into Gorillas. They protect it with all their might. I was willing to earn my freedom at any cost. Knock yourself out.

You can't keep a good man down for too long. Not this 'good' man. I had been in the domestic prison too long. In a golden cage with an open door now?

14

SOUTH OF THE BORDER

I soon bounced back with a vengeance. Bachelor life started all over again with gusto. I was incorrigible. I resurrected the business successfully and went wild, drinking, smoking pot and visiting prostitutes, hookers, escorts, whores, call girls- the professionals. It all started with massages, the gateway. Bodily pleasures escalated gradually, and I ended up visiting professional escorts. Two three hundred dollars would light up your day. Fuck frugality. I had so much money that few hundred here and there made no difference.

It was as if there were no tomorrow, as if the world were coming to an end—Armageddon—and I had to hurry and have as much adult fun as I could. In other words, fuck as many women as I could. A new girl every other day or so. My peers were aghast at my lifestyle, blown way. I love women, every aspect of them.

Then I met Ann. She and I would check out the swinger scene. I thought I had died and fucked my way to heavens. Swinger lifestyle is extreme fucking sport.

The Internet opened up a new world of possibilities. I couldn't believe the amount of pornography I discovered online, the number of female escorts that were available for hire through various websites. All types of women were advertised for sale— or should I say FOR RENT. From sexpots in suggestive poses to sweet looking girl-next-door types, their photos were plastered all over the cyberspace. All you needed were a few franklins and an erection. The call girls were temporarily yours for your pleasure, but for a price. I was loaded.

After I had exhausted the local talent, I hit L.A. where women from all corners of the globe were available for the carnal consumption. The Russians had invaded America with this fine export. If KGB are cold killers, these communist chicks are ice cold fuckers.

Enter Viagra, the blue pill. My landlord at work introduced me to this miracle pill that would turbocharge the debauchery. After going through the women in the States, I started traveling all over the world looking for Sex. As usual, I had clarity what I wanted. I looked on the Internet to determine where in the world a bachelor should go to have adult Fun. There must have been a trillion websites catering to the perverted, disturbed, sick men, or, simply put, men who wanted to screw someone other than their spouse. What's wrong with that? Smiles. I was like a kid in a candy store. I thought *Hey, you only live once.* Having no financial, religious or moral compunctions, I wanted to fuck as many women as I could. I wonder if I instinctively knew of the impending doom?

I have always been very conscious of staying in top shape. Our bodies are glorious creations. They ought to be respected and honored. Regular exercise, a balanced diet, and sufficient sleep are three of the easiest ways to increase our passion, energy and enthusiasm for life. Physical well-being is the foundation upon which a healthy life is built. People spend too much time and energy following this or that diet, whereas all they need is a little bit of discipline and common sense. Most diet lifestyles are a joke.

I took weeks off and played with the South Americans, body surfing and partying like a rock star, like an animal. I went to Costa Rica, then to Rio de Janeiro, Brazil, where I had one of the greatest times of my life for a month. The dizzying array of vegetables, sweets, and fruits were a dream come true for this flexitarian who generally likes veggies and fruits, but will eat pussy and fish occasionally. Did I say pussy, sorry, I meant poultry.

The tiny island of Curaçao in the Dutch Antilles is a peculiar place. Unbelievable! This interesting island, just north of Caracas, Venezuela, is a special place worth mentioning. There is nothing like it in the world, If you are into that sort of thing. Prostitution is legal in Curaçao. There was once a large military base there. The entire base has been turned into a giant open air Brothel called Le Mirage, aka Campo Alegre.

Le Mirage has hundreds of tiny dormitories on the property. A wide variety of girls from South America, Eastern Europe and elsewhere pose seductively in the doorways, showing off their false tits, tummy tucks, facelifts, soliciting customers from all over the world to partake in the sins of the flesh. You pay a $25 fee to enter this former military base turned whorehouse, then you are free to walk around and pick the 'Candy' of your choice. For a nominal tip, you get to be her guest until you are... 'Happy.'

Curaçao attracts European customers who come in droves on nonstop transatlantic chartered flights, especially from Netherlands (now I know why they are the happiest nations in the world.) Italians are everywhere, so are Germans, Belgians, and French. Curaçao competes with Havana and Rio de Janeiro for the major skin trade. For all you ballers out there, if you are fortunate enough to be reading this: In my opinion, of all the places I've been, Rio de Janeiro is the hands down winner in the skin trade competition. The 'Termas' in Catholic Brazil are unofficial whorehouses. Beautiful but poor Portuguese-speaking women from the favelas (barrios) are eager to trade skin for money.

The favelas are densely populated areas along the hillsides where poverty, drugs, crime and violence are rampant. Until recently, even the police wouldn't dare go there. They are self-governed fiefdoms, ruled by local crime lords. I was advised by my hotel staff, Not to go there. Those places are not safe, even for local residents, let alone tourists. And what did adventurous me do? I took a bus and walked right into the most notorious favela, in the heart of Rio, not too far from the giant statue of Christ the Redeemer, which is the largest Art Deco statue in the world and a symbol of Brazilian Christianity.

The damn hypocrisy of religiosity is so palpable around the world. It is one thing to be nonreligious and indulge in such episodes. But it is flat out wrong when you hypocritically claim to be a believer and then flagrantly violate the teachings of the religion, that requires you not to indulge. Then you choose to flout those commands. Oh, nigga, please don't even get me started on this subject. Brazil's Catholics claim to be a pious people and display the statue of a giant Jesus overlooking Rio while allowing the skin trade to flourish openly, shamelessly. Pope needs to visit Brazil more often.

I took a casual stroll on the narrow and steep winding streets of this favela. The place had a mind-boggling maze of alleys teeming with poor, hungry, thuggish looking rough people. I elicited menacing stares, glares and even some smiles from the locals. Word must have spread that there was a brown fool in town. I sat with the local hoodlums and had a few beers. Language was a barrier, limiting conversation.

Portuguese is not an easy language to speak or learn, and the locals did not understand English. I returned to the hotel safely.

When I told the hotel staff where I had spent the day, they rolled their eyes and shook their heads. They had seen chicks come and go in my room as if there was a beauty contest being held in the hotel. Hotel policy did not permit working girls on the premises, so I had to bribe my hosts to look the other way, while I would be going thru the blue pills rapidly.

I had a great time in Brazil. I traveled up and down the coast. Brazil's natural beauty and sandy beaches are some of the best in the world.

The country is a smorgasbord of exotic women and delicious fruits and vegetables that are indigenous to Brazil only. I was in heaven. I caught some of the best body surfing waves not too far from the world famous Copacabana Beach.

Brazil is relatively inexpensive to visit, and the locals welcome foreign tourists, although Americans are seen as overbearing and rude warmongers. The poverty is heartbreaking in this huge South American country. Brazilians are a proud people, simple and industrious. I found that they were weary and somewhat uninformed about the United States. They were unhappy with our past trigger-happy war policies in that part of the world. We did leave a bad impression with our past para-military misadventures in Chile, Colombia, Grenada, Guatemala and elsewhere.

Cuba did not welcome me with open arms. I wanted to spend a month or so in Cuba to play, but I cut my visit short and wanted to get the hell out of Havana. I couldn't; there were no flights out. Inbound flight were half empty, outbound were full. I felt once in, there is no way out. I felt trapped.

Well, let me relive the nightmare. The trip began happily and innocently. I thought it was going to be a little adventure. I took a flight out of Montego Bay, Jamaica. I had two suitcases. One held my belongings and the other was packed with gifts for the locals, including chick stuff. A trusted friend told me to take feminine trinkets, like lipstick, makeup, and lotions. I would be warmly welcomed by women, for bringing in banned items.

Being a voracious reader, I had a half-dozen books with me and about seven or eight thousand dollars cash. Hey, I'm a high roller, and I was there to play and that costs money ... Smiles. The customs agents at Havana Airport did not like me. They were stumped by the items in my luggage. I was thoroughly interrogated and searched. Air Jamaica had landed at 9 p.m., and I was there until 3 a.m. being questioned by a few frowning Cuban agents who did not speak English. Bastards did not have an interpreter either. I had a Spanish to English dictionary, but that didn't help much. There was a complete communication breakdown.

The Cuban agents suspected that I was there for some nefarious purpose, like corrupting their youth with my books. I did my best to convince them that I was there to play, wink wink; therefore, I was carrying a wad of cash. I also told them that I was a scholar. I was interested in reading and writing. I was not there to corrupt their youth; I was there to get corrupted, you monkeys. To spend money, spread wealth, fuck.

They had me convert all my dollars into Cuban pesos at the airport, thereby instantly losing 20 percent in exchange value. Then they wanted me not to stay at the swanky hotel of my liking but at a dump of their choice, where I would have to stay for at least three days. I said, "Whatever, dude, just let me go so I can eat and sleep." I took a taxi to the hotel and paid a million pesos to the cabbie who took me for a ride that seemed to last forever. After I had checked in, I went to my room and slept—under watchful eyes.

The supermarkets had half-empty shelves, restaurants had limited menus, with only a few fruits. I seldom saw any late model cars on the streets, only old classic American cars from the sixties, belching smoke. I felt that I had traveled back in the time machine, which may be novel for some, not me.

The Cuban girls were not as attractive as I expected. They were mostly mixed race or black, very willing to sell their bodies, dirt cheap. Plainclothes cops were everywhere. On top of it all, the beaches were not that good for body surfing. No waves. I had to travel for hours before finding any decent waves.

As feared by the local authorities, I engaged the youth and corrupted them with my chitchat. Not many of them wanted to talk openly. They warned me that EL Supremo was watching and listening. Paranoia? I met one young Cuban, who told me that he had spent seven years in prison because he had attempted to escape to the United States in a boat and gotten caught by Cuban coast guard. The general population, except for the old guard, wanted Fidel Castro to die peacefully, thus paving way for Cuba to step up to the challenges of the twenty-first century.

I stood in a line for everything. I mean every fucking thing, be it a grocery store, ice cream parlor, dance club, cafes, bus or taxi stops. I went to the airline office and, what else, stood in a line and begged the airline clerks to get me out of this wretched place. Finally, I got confirmation from Air Jamaica notifying me that I had a seat on a flight to get me out of Gitmo. The place made me sick. I did, however, like the architecture, especially the world famous opera houses, and the historical monuments.

The Cuban girls were cheap but scared shitless of getting caught. I did meet a girl and had a short and sweet affair with her. She wanted to come to America. She begged me to sponsor her. I felt sorry for her and all the others trapped on that island prison. Fuck that horrible socialist experiment. I will take capitalism any day.

Back on Moonlight Beach in California, I hooked up with a twenty-five-year-old enchanter who kept me energized and out of trouble. I met Dar while shopping in the local weekend bazaar. I was dressed as a transvestite, wearing red lipstick and a purple wig, with my fingernails and toenails polished in Rasta colors. It was Sunday, my daring day of fun and games. I loved the stares, the shocked and dismayed looks that I got from most, except women. Some younger women dig older men, father figure? After a few weeks, I asked her out. We became inseparable. We dated for six months or so, until that night. I was beginning to fall in love, even admitting to her the day before the shooting. She was wide-eyed.

Dar is a white girl of average height with dark hair. She is attractive and easy going and a very sweet, open-minded free spirit. We had terrific chemistry, both sexual and spiritual. She went to school and ran a perfume shop in funky Encinitas on weekends. She loved life and was open to experimentation. She lived with her sister but spent most nights with me. We had a very active sex life fueled by Viagra, ganja, and stimulating conversations. But despite the relationship with Dar, I visited hookers, though infrequently. I told you I was a sick puppy, a sex addict.

Dar had beautiful, shoulder-length, black curly hair. One evening, during seduction, I asked if she would ever cut her hair as I like short hair on girls, the lean, boyish look. She looked deeply into my eyes and asked me if I had any scissors. Fuck me. I ran over and gave her the scissors I used for cutting my pubic hair. She sat in front of my closet mirror and, lo and behold, started cutting her cherished hair, inch by inch, layer by layer, to neck level. It blew me away. That night we must have had the best sex ever. Dar was at my place the night of the home invasion robbery.

I continued to see my Ex-wife and had a remarkable relationship with my daughters who had gone off to college in Santa Barbara and were having the time of their lives. I had made a deal with my daughters. As long as they stayed in college and got good grades, I would support them, paying for everything. I did not ask for them to be high achievers, only that they study, live happy and content lives.

They are two very interesting young ladies, my source of inspiration and my incentive to be safe, strong and prosperous. The very sight, or even the thought of my daughters fills me up with joy. The gods have been very kind to me in giving me these two precious gifts from the heavens—or wherever, forever!

I always tell others to stay motivated and occupied with their chosen professions and hobbies or with life in general and to make sure that their actions are consistent with their objectives. Focus on your bottom lines like a laser beam. At the end of the day, life should be about happiness first. Keep this in mind, have it engraved somewhere: You are the governor of your life. Even when you misgovern, you are still the chief architect, builder, banker and maker of your circumstances, maybe even your damn destiny.

As for me, in 2006, I was somewhere in my fifties, at the peak of a wonderful journey, dating an attractive lover, with whom I had good chemistry despite the age difference. I was giddy with life, but my fascinating lifelong luck was about to run out. I was getting sloppy, careless, even stupid.

My pad was on a public street on Moonlight Beach. Public beaches attract all kinds of people, including riffraff. Rock and R&B tunes were always blasting out on my patio. I was probably flashing money, driving expensive cars in questionable neighborhoods, having wild parties at my beach pad and running around with shady characters.

I openly smoked pot and courted whores, in Addition to Dar, Ann, my Ex, and others. Even gods must have been getting jealous. Chicks were in and out of my place so often, I should have had a revolving door. Arrogance, intolerance, and insolence may have been creeping in. Master of the universe? All good things must end? The bubble was about to burst. Not with a pinprick but with a fucking Gunshot.

15

APRIL FOOL

APRIL Fools Day 2006 was a fateful day. That date is written on my mind forever. That night changed my life forever, for the worse. The higher you go, the harder you fall. Life was simply too good; it was unreal, a fairytale life like Princess Diana. Something had to give. The Princess is dead and this Prince was about to be shot.

Around sunset, my neighbor came over. Devin lived across the alley. I had a beer with him and smoked herb. He saw an ounce of marijuana sitting on my table, which I had bought earlier from a first-time source. Devin and I chatted about inane, superficial stuff. He left thereafter.

Dar came over with groceries for us to make dinner. Well, she made it, I watched—I don't cook. I drank another beer and got stoned with her. We had an outstanding evening of dance, romance, and intense lovemaking. Around 10 p.m., I wanted to go to bed. Dar said her back was stiff and that she would rather lie on the hard floor of the living room for a short while, for me to go ahead and go to bed; she would join me shortly. I kissed her, thanked her for fucking my brains out, she said the pleasure was all hers. I retired to the bedroom.

I woke up around midnight, perhaps to go to the bathroom. I could have heard a noise, I don't know. I had a one bedroom apartment with the bedroom opening onto a narrow corridor. The bathroom was to my right and the kitchen and living room to my left. I had left the bedroom door slightly ajar. I don't lock any doors. As I opened the bedroom door half asleep, I saw a muscular white man right in my face, like 12 inches away, screaming in a shrill tone. He wore makeup, a clown hat, and heavy glitter. He was startled to see me.

The 'Clown' reminded me of the Joker, the psychopathic comic book character played by Heath Ledger in the movie *The Dark Knight*. Was this an April Fool's prank? I might have muttered "What the fuck?" and instinctively lunged at the intruder. I remember hearing a muffled sound, like a shot from a gun with a silencer. I felt a hot, oily feeling in my neck, things went dark. The bullet had pierced my throat next to the Adams apple and got lodged in my spinal cord at the back of my neck.

I fell back on my ass from the force of the bullet. The lights went out. I have a vague memory of trying to rise and falling back, almost fainting. There was no pain, just nothingness, dark, which would get worse. I heard some noises, and the next thing I remember, I was in Dar's lap. I heard her sobbing, "Oh God, oh God, oh God, what should I do?" I remember saying, "Call 9-1-1." My muffled, husky whisper reminded me of Marlon Brando in the movie 'Godfather.'

I remotely heard the paramedics saying soothing things, and I vaguely remember seeing the flashing red lights of the ambulance. I remember wondering where was Devin, as my stretcher passed his apartment. I was taken to the hospital nearby. In the ambulance, I heard a voice that seemed far away, "Hang tough, Bro. We will get you to the hospital shortly, stay with me." I knew I was toast. Ouch!

Devin, a recent transplant from Philadelphia, lived a stone's throw away from my apartment; His kitchen window faced my living room across the alley. He was in his early forties, a blonde, muscular surfer who often wore silver fingernail and toenail polish and matching earrings. Devin had a troubled history, but no one really knew much about him. He loved the Internet, metal rock, drugs and guns. We visited each other's beach pads and went surfing once. Devin lived alone, but his out of town, glamorous girlfriend would come to stay with him for weeks.

Sometimes she came over to my place to bitch about her life with him and seek my counsel. Sometimes she had a drink or got stoned with me. I had no interest in her. She was his girlfriend; I had no intention of banging her. Zero. I am built that way. I told her what I would tell anyone else who asked my opinion: to live a life of dignity and self-respect, and do not let anyone insult, hurt or rule you. I was just trying to help.

Devin had confided to me earlier that he had some trouble with the law. He told me he was behind on bills, including child support and alimony payments. He had to come up with $10,000 right away or else he would go to jail. He was supposedly late on paying child support to a previous wife. Perhaps it was a lie. Who knows? He was always short on cash and overdue on bills. He asked to borrow ten grand from me. What else is new? I flatly refused to lend him money. I may have added insult to injury, "Are you kidding me? Not lending you $10. You are a loser, man."

Several loans that I have made in my life, mostly to family members, have gone sour. Not only did I lose money, I also lost relationships. Debtors avoid you like they would a bill collector. Most people who know me knew that I kept large amounts of cash on me. A stupid native habit. Devin knew it too, everyone did. I kept many thousands of dollars in cash stashed in unsuspecting places, like in a jar, tucked behind clothing, behind the washing machine. Anywhere but under the mattress, duh. I trust people.

Moonlight Beach was a very friendly neighborhood. Six or seven of us tenants from different units would hang out, drink, eat, dance, smoke and watch beautiful sunsets over the ocean. We all had parties. Our candlelit apartments, with music filtering out, were always open. I rarely locked my door. I still don't.

An Australian chick by the name of Diva lived next door above Devin's apartment. I frequently visited her apartment as she was sweet, scholarly with a sharp wit, and her apartment had a better view of the sunsets over the water. I told Diva about Devin wanting to borrow money and warned them that he might hit her up with money request too. We all agreed that he was kind of questionable and not to be trusted with a loan that large.

Diva, a very delightful soul in her fifties, came to visit me in ICU and would later tell me that she had lent him the money out of the goodness of her heart (and perhaps to get laid?) I am sure she asked him not to mention it to me as I had cautioned her not to fall for his con. Well, if so, then he must have been righteously furious that I was muddying the waters for him And that I was banging his girlfriend, which I was not. I don't fuck chicks with large fake tits. Sorry!

Devin was the last guy to see me that evening. He had come by my place. He saw the large bag of weed. He knew I carried cash. Did he leave only to return? The stars must have been lining up for my life to turn shitty forever.

We are talking Encinitas, a well-to-do, artsy, folksy, laid-back beach city, the yoga center of California, where nothing like that ever occurs. It's all about peace, love, and sex around here. People are socializing on every corner. The area is literally crawling with cops to maintain law and order. Interestingly the shooting was not even mentioned in local papers, perhaps to maintain the real estate values.

The paramedics must have come within minutes; they rushed me to the emergency room of Scripps Hospital, ten minutes away.

I was barely alive, with an oxygen mask over my face. I heard voices calling my name and a voice saying, "Breath, breath." I wondered who were they calling; they were mispronouncing my name. It had to be me. I must be seriously injured.

No problem. My sunny disposition went into top gear *'Eh minor, I will be treated and released.* From Encinitas, I was transferred to the ICU, the intensive care unit, at the main Scripps Hospital in La Jolla where I would stay for over three months, mostly on a ventilator with a tracheotomy. After that, I spent another three months undergoing rehabilitation at a different hospital. It was a nightmare. My body had gone into a shock, shut down; I was immobile.

The next day, I had neck surgery, followed by several other complex surgeries with unfamiliar medical names, including, but not limited to, surgery for a punctured lung, a tracheotomy, gall bladder removal, a spinal fusion and more. For days, my body temperature wouldn't go below 102 degrees. Cold would be a killer. The doctors were stumped. I would feel Ice cold for months to come, shivering, driving everyone nuts.

The doctors had me undergo several CAT scans, daily chest X-rays, and several MRIs to find the source of the high fever. Finally, they zeroed in on the infected gall bladder. Spinal cord was severed. Doctors would regularly put a ventilator on my face and hang me upside down to remove the phlegm. The tracheotomy would be my companion for six months. Spine was fused with titanium rods.

I was told that I would not walk again. Fuck. It happens to people all the time. I guess it was just my turn. There ought to be a law Not to save a life if the injury is so severe that one will be dependent on others and be a burden to society forever. Good for friends and family, sure. They don't have to suffer the severe pain for the rest of their lives, but not good for

147

the injured, who has to suffer the indignities of being invalid and live a martyr's life. I think if you can't take a dump on your own, You need to check out. Adios! Only a healthy life is a good life. Everyone talks about saving lives. Strangely no one talks about the quality of life saved. Wouldn't you agree? Perhaps not.

I had no enemies who would want me dead or even hurt. I have not knowingly caused irreparable harm to anyone in last three decades or so. Yes, I have been shoddy, slippery, careless, and reckless, may be a rich fuck to some. Someone could have been jealous or held a grudge, but not insofar that he or she would want me dead.

I cannot put my finger on anyone, or even point my finger toward anyone, but the main suspect. Could it be an angry pimp or the ex-spouse of one of the few chicks I was banging. It was not a hit. I am reasonably certain that it was a robbery by an acquaintance who wanted money, even revenge.

He did not come intending to kill me. I think the shooter was high, perhaps on meth. I startled him in the doorway. I lunged at him instinctively (wouldn't you?) and the gun went off. What I cannot explain is this: My girlfriend Dar, who was sleeping in the living room, told the investigators that she heard a noise and woke up to see two or maybe three people approaching her. One of them took her purse, asked her to be quiet and left, running away. She didn't have her contact lenses on, and she is as blind as a bat without contacts. Go figure.

A police investigation followed. The lead detective, a portly sergeant, came to the ICU and interviewed me. He had me help the sketch artist draw a picture of the suspect. The policeman seemed lackadaisical and indifferent. Maybe because during his investigation he saw an ounce of ganja, cash, a bong and a few books on the Mafia (The Colombian Billionaire Escobar and Mexican kingpin El Chapo) in my room, leading him to assume that I was dirty.

The Sergeant served a search warrant on Devin's place and even traveled to Cleveland where Devin had previously lived. Kevin owned a gun similar to the one that was used in the shooting. He claimed he had lost the gun a while back. Surprise. The detective, who was not exactly Sherlock, submitted his report and advised the D.A to issue a warrant for Devin's arrest.

Six months later, I got a call from the D.A that took me by total surprise. I couldn't believe what I heard. She informed me that there was insufficient evidence to charge Devin. The state couldn't indict him. To prosecute Devin and put him away for twenty years would require proof beyond a shadow of a doubt. There was no solid technological or corroborative evidence to justify an indictment. There were no reliable witnesses, no hair fibers, no fingerprints, no DNA and no gun.

I must have been silent for a long time. She called out my name twice. I was stunned, I heard her say that I probably could get a judgment against him in a civil court where the burden of proof is not as heavy. Say, like in the case of OJ Simpson. OJ could not be convicted in a criminal court but was successfully tried and convicted in a civil court.

I was surprised and disappointed, but also stoic and calm. To sue him meant dragging people in the courtroom, serving subpoenas to witnesses like Dar, which was not acceptable to me. I hate to re-live the incident. I am a total believer in the American- and natural- justice system, Karma. The same system that had declined to indict me thirty-five years ago when I killed a man in self-defense had declined to indict my shooter.

I do not hold a grudge against the system, the D.A or Devin. Shit happens. That's the way things roll. I did not cry out for justice or revenge. I was neither angry nor bitter, and I did not seek retribution, much to the surprise and dismay of my loved ones, especially my daughters who were beside themselves. I never saw them as upset, angry and disappointed.

Getting shot and being hospitalized was a surreal experience. People tell me that I suffered from paranoid hallucinations for a few days. What I went through, I would not wish upon my worst enemies: On a ventilator, confined to a cold hospital bed. On my back, unable to turn or move. On morphine, with tubes coming out from everywhere in my body. Poohing and peeing in bed, having others wipe me. Having to be fed through tubes, breathing uneasily, Uncertain of my surroundings. The real killer was water. I was not allowed to even take a sip for months.

I was fighting for my life, not knowing what the future would hold. It was unreal in the sense that for days I really thought I had died and that I was now dealing with another world. My recurring thought was, *Why are they trying so hard; why are they trying like hell to Save me? You damn well know that I will always be crippled. That I forever will be seeing you stupid doctors who were gleefully stitching me together.* Doctors must love to see people fried, gives 'em work.

The bright side was seeing family and friends coalescing around my sick body. I loved seeing my three chicks lying with me, refusing to leave my bedside against hospital rules. My ex-wife was distraught but determined to keep me alive. I fell in love with her for the first time in my life. What an incredible trooper she is, along with Sheila and Geena.

That first night, I awoke in the ICU heavily dosed with morphine and a bunch of other pills with weird names that started with letters like *Z* or *X*. This one doctor came in and asked me Whom I wanted as my guardian? Who should have the final say in my affairs regarding money, life, death and other doomsday scenarios? No one knew if I was going to live or die for several weeks. Dude, it was Unreal. My ex-wife and my girlfriend, Dar were both in the waiting room, sobbing. Everyone was upset, distraught, crying. My two brothers, TG and RG and several relatives from L.A. would regularly drive a hundred miles south on interstate 5 to be with us.

It took me a split second to navigate through the morphine-induced confusion to choose my Ex as my guardian, perhaps disappointing Dar who was equally upset and scared. She thought the shooter might come back for her as she was the only witness, and the invaders had her purse with her ID in it. Concerned, she moved to Northern California soon after.

Rediscovering the Ex would become a phenomenal experience. I would genuinely try to become her lover and her best friend. I really bent over backward to make it work. Man, it's hard. It worked for a while but not for long. Underlying fissures persisted..

All my life I had lived like a rock star, dancing, laughing and living a full life. I couldn't believe that the bubble had not Yet burst. Well, it finally did burst, with a... damn gunshot.

16

GUNSHOT

Since that evening, life has not been worth living. I would rather scoop out my eyes with a rusty spoon than to relive the last eight plus years. It's been pure hell, full of physical pain, mental confusion and a feeling of helplessness. I'm in a wheelchair and totally dependent on others. Caregivers are not in my league. They are expensive and unreliable, and some of them steal. I have often thought about checking out, and were it not for my lovely girls, I would have done so long ago. Should one live in pain and misery so loved ones are happy that you are around or should one check out and let them learn to live with their loss? So far I have chosen, martyrdom misery and pain for myself.

Constantly dealing with hospitals, doctors, pharmacies, medications, and caregivers is mundane, sterile, repetitive and frustrating. I suffer from terrible nerve pain in my ass. Apparently, the force of the gunshot caused major trauma to nerves, confusing and confounding their functions. Bladder infections are omnipresent. I am a paraplegic, paralyzed from the nipple line down. I have a piss bag that I carry like a lunch box on me all the time, the result of a catheter inserted above the pelvis. Defecating is a major ordeal and only successful when a suppository is inserted up my rectum. Swallowing and breathing are difficult. My fingers don't work except the middle finger, and my hands ache and burn.

My voice box doesn't function as one of the two vocal cords is severed. The damn bullet went right through it and got lodged in the spinal column. It takes much energy just to talk; finally my words come out in a Godfather-like whisper.

The undying love and compassion of my women is beyond description. They were in my room 24/7, defying hospital rules, snuggling up to me and keeping my body warm. The nurses had never seen such heavy traffic of well-wishers coming and going. They would frequently tell me how lucky I was to have them in my life. Get the fuck out. You call this good fortune?

I did go back to work selling airplanes in October 2006, six months after the incident. I work every day, seven days a week. I can work the keyboard with one finger. On the positive side, as my muscles weaken, my resolve gets stronger; as my speech slows, my writing gets stronger; as I am diminished physically, I swear to be stronger mentally and emotionally. I may be down, but I'm not defeated. The yogi, Julia told a common friend that she heard I had been killed. I guess "the rumors of my death have been greatly exaggerated," to quote Mark Twain.

People ought to treat handicap people as equals and not give them any special treatment or sympathy. When we, the disabled, come across you, it's best to treat us as if we were normal. A courteous display of compassion is natural, thank you, but please don't fawn over us. It is unwarranted as it will remind us of our inadequacies that we are trying to forget and feel normal. We Know you have pity, sorrow or empathy and that you are only trying to help.

Most of us will ask for help if it is needed. So, please back off with your generosity of spirit, however genuine. Fuck you... I mean thank you... another big smile. When you see disabled persons, train your eyes not to look at them with pity, and don't look away either and pretend we don't exist. We do, it's just that we've been cut in half.

I have a power chair and an electrical bed, and my van is fitted with an electrical ramp. I need care most of the time. I can't turn over in bed on my own. Someone has to turn me in the middle of the night. I would likely develop skin issues, like bed sores if I were not turned over. I do continue to carry on a normal life as I have to provide for my family whose love, care and support sustains me and keeps me from throwing myself in front of a train. I don't know how long I can bear this life. Not that long, I hope, or should I say, I promise.

To be honest, I don't mind telling you that I came close to it a couple of times. Amtrak was the hands-down winner.

Now, I don't know about you, but I never cared to be famous, big or be remembered posthumously, like having my name inscribed on a wall and shit. I will be quite happy to exit without being Mr. Somebody. Fame, fortune, titles and worldly possessions have never impressed me. I don't care to leave a legacy or be remembered. None!

Most of all, being an alleged Sexaholic all my life, I have lost my huge desire to have sex as I don't feel much in the lower torso. Nature must rearrange physical and psychological abilities and make one compatible with the other. My entire life revolved around women, sexuality, seduction and eroticism. All of it is gone. I am trying to get my mojo back.

Most of the time, life seems boring, barren, flat and almost useless. Lack of faith or religious belief could be one reason. If I believed in God or Allah or gave myself up to Jesus Christ as my savior—as many people in distress do, and That is a fact ladies and gentlemen—having faith may have made me more resilient and hopeful than I am. They say hope is the last thing to die. I feel hopeless and helpless to boot. I seem to have lost my anchor, my compass and, more importantly, my once voracious appetite, libido. Sexuality doesn't do much to me anymore, nothing, Zero!

In my view, severely handicapped people are a drain on society. People treat you with extra attention and compassion, always reminding you that you are not normal, a victim, not like everybody else, that you are a man with Special needs. A longing for true affection, coupled with recurring thoughts on the futility of this state of life, nags me more often than not. Being vulnerable and in need of comfort, help and understanding confuses me as I have been on the other side as the one dishing out advice and methods for living a full and fulfilled life.

When asked by inquirers, my answer always had been that I lived the best life I knew, and I sincerely meant it. Friends would be taken aback when I said that.

Then the most beautiful life I had always lived took an ominous turn. Shit happens to people all the time, just pick up your local paper or turn on your TV or your smart phone. I guess now I have to take the good with the bad and stop self-flagellating. As I often say to people, "Deal with it. Elvis has left the building." Do I have a bad attitude? Maybe.

I have to remind myself that it's pointless to wallow in the past or worry about the future. Just focus on taking care of the present moment—each moment is a lifetime. When you take care of the present moment, it takes care of the next moment and, in turn, the next hour, the next day, next month or next life? (Next life, you believe that shit?) So if you take care of today, you would be taking care of tomorrow, which invariably comes. Plan things so that each moment takes care of the next. Regret and guilt are our deadly twin enemies, I repeat.

It is in your best interest to advertise your true self so that only the right kinds of customers are attracted to you. Eventually, truth and reality prevails. As the Reggae star Bob Marley sang, "You can fool some people some of the time, but you can't fool all the people all the time." Intellectual honesty, inevitability, and integrity are hard to come by. Cultivate it, face it and magic will appear. If you are completely honest with yourself and admit who you really are to yourself and others, you will find peace and harmony within your soul. Wise, thoughtful folks will respect you for that.

Life has been a great ride. Yes, I Am controversial and contradictory, and I am irreverent of social mores and values. I am also a very strong advocate of my firm beliefs, and I have the courage of my convictions. My skeptical, bold, caustic and critical approach to matters turns off many people. I appear intimidating to some. I wish I cared.

I seek confident and well-grounded company to mingle, match and reason. I research issues and become well informed before I opine on the subject. Once you catch my drift and accept the sincere scrutiny that is my bedrock, we likely will become lifelong friends. I guarantee it. Or maybe you don't want to be my friend; I am cool with that. I may not be cut out for you. Beauty is in the eye of the beholder.

I have developed strong and lasting friendships. Some of my good friends still get mad at me because of my irreverence, indiscretion and transparency to a fault. Many urge me to be kinder, gentler and less judgmental. Heaven knows, I try but fail. I seem to piss off some people, even close friends. When people get mad at their loved ones, what do they usually do? They cry foul and cut off the offender, at least temporarily, which I find retarded, insecure and weak. One does not need many friends, anyway, just a few good ones.

Some criticize me for being Too analytical, insensitive and invasive, thinking that I am the grand inquisitor. It is not in my nature to be otherwise, but I continue to work at becoming more sensitive and less intrusive. I secretly wish though that people would steal themselves and stand up to the critical scrutiny of an inquiring mind of a friend. Grow some skin.

When I ask meaningful questions about your life, I am sincerely trying to be your friend. Allow me to ask tough questions, please. There is a method to my madness. I am weighing whether we can be friends. My time is precious, just like yours. My inquiries have a reason. We are all in this thing called 'life' together. I want to understand you, help you and share my life recipes with you. I ask you to do the same so it helps us grow together. That to me is true friendship. That is my mission.

Everyone has a purpose in life, a gift from the makers. What is yours? Mine is to help you and all those whose lives intersect and interact with mine in any way. I want to be a bridge to your destination, which may be different from mine. I feel qualified and sufficiently educated to be helpful and judgmental in one's quest for life.

Those who say one cannot be judgmental are wrong. We make judgments all the time. On daily basis, it is our duty to assess, analyze and ascertain—Judge—what to do and what not to do. In the aircraft sales business. I have to make snap decisions—judgments. I have to know whom to trust and whom not to trust. If I don't know that, I will fail. Our time and cash are on the line; we may want to weed out the bullshitters and the posers. You making an informed decision- judgment - is critical. You owe it to yourself. Doing that is not judging in a negative or derogative way.

I have lived a full life, as opposed to standing on the sidelines and watching life pass by. I have not been afraid to take the initiative and explore, experiment, take action, gamble and take calculated risks, then let the chips fall where they may. Furthermore, I do not wish ill to anyone or anything, even the fucking assassin. My conscious is as clear as a summer day is long.

17

SEX

Of the seven cardinal sins, I have had a relatively easy time dealing with six of them: Anger, sloth, pride, gluttony, greed and envy. I have deliciously failed on the seventh cardinal sin, Lust, my Achilles heel. Growing up in a repressive and segregated society where men and women are kept away from each other must have led to my excessive, pent up desires and longings.

I have had an incredibly huge and voracious sexual appetite. I have tirelessly battled this beautiful, but dangerous addiction, which almost took me to the brink numerous times, endangering my life, liberty and pursuit of pussy... err, I meant happiness. You don't want to know the details, although the statute of limitations has expired on most of my escapades. Maybe I just don't care anymore. Keep reading, the devil is in the details.

I have had a hard-on for females ever since I can remember. No one, no chick was out of bounds, except family members and big- booty ugly black and huge Samoan mammas. Most women have been fair game. I think every chick is someone's daughter. Mine is not any more special than or different from yours. I really meant no harm; I just wanted to be with selective women sexually and to enjoy the fine art of seduction.

I think this world would be a better place if more people were fucking. Justice and equality must rule. I was an equal opportunity fucker. If it wasn't for the gunshot, who knows what my fate would have been. Since the Lorena Bobbitt affair, I have been afraid of getting my ham sliced too, Smiles. My often risky sexual behavior defies logic and reason. My lascivious conduct is regarded as immoral by most cultures and religions. I am sorry for the excesses and the hurt I may have inflicted in the heat of the moment, like a dog in heat. I sincerely apologize to all, especially to my benefactor or tormentor, my ex-wife.

I must have spent an ungodly sum of money, time, and energy, traveling to the ends of the earth seeking women of all colors, creed, race, and shape to quench my never-ending thirst. Several years ago, the Internet opened up endless and shameless ways to score women. I have had countless encounters—hundreds—and without contracting any diseases. Thank you. Sounds strange, but it's true.

I remember the day of my surgery at Scripps Hospital, a staff member brought a psychologist, a somber priest and some papers to sign. One of the forms was a consent to be tested for the AIDS virus. Fuck. My mind did a somersault. What if? They had to test me for the feared disease before they took me to the operating room. I guess they take appropriate steps in case the patient is infected. I thought, oh shit, the moment of truth finally had arrived.

AIDS was something that I had feared like an audit. During my partying years, I regularly had myself tested for venereal diseases for which there are cures. I never checked for AIDS because there is no cure for this deadly virus. So, my rationale was, why check for something that has no known cure?

I had no choice but to sign a consent form, wondering if I may have contracted the disease during the years I bedded women all over the world. The result that came back was a pleasant surprise and a huge relief. Negative. No AIDS. Phew! Wearing condom paid off? or was it my mom's prayers. The latter? Get outta here.

No, luck had nothing to do with it. It was me- cautious, obsessed with cleanliness. I look at the teeth, the nails. The smell, the aroma (or the stink) of the body. I can smell from miles. Bad breath is a dead giveaway. If you stink, my alarm bells start ringing. What did you do to stink like that, Jesus. Paying $300 or so would generally ensure a clean escort.

Safe sex was a major factor in not contracting any disease, not luck. Fuck the luck. Luck is opportunity meeting preparation. If you have the right information, connections and resources, then luck comes knocking at your door. Don't you think that the harder and smarter you work, the luckier you get.

I have used condoms with everyone, even with my own wife who is practically a nun sans me. Each encounter made the next one more exciting, more erotic. Variety was king. The anticipation, the novelty and the suspense of the new Meet (not Meat, you pervert) went beyond the high of any drug. Every time I had a new escort arrive, it was like opening a new Christmas present. I did all my diligence on the phone, Before the meeting. Ask relevant questions, qualify 'em so you have a good idea, what you getting. Be careful what you ask on the phone, as it may be admissible in court.

One time I asked just Too many questions from a decoy on the telephone. Vice was listening in and used it as a corroborating evidence to cuff me.

Prostitution and sex trafficking have gone way beyond any-one's imagination. The Internet has brought these professions into every home and office. Yes, there is sleaze, trash and abuse in abundance, but I'm talking class and elegance: professional hookers with the images of a girl next door gone wild. Married men who choose to get involved in affairs for whatever reasons may be making a mistake. To keep the marriage from failing, it is best Not to have affairs, especially An affair.

Emotional involvement with another woman would not only be threatening, but possibly fatal to any fledgling marriage, the final nail in the coffin. The old idiom "Hell hath no fury like a woman scorned" is true. She will eat (not that kind, see you keep going there) you alive. As such, I surmised that it is best to Pay for sex. That way, there is no personal involvement, no strings attached. You never have to see that woman again.

This may sound chauvinistic, sexist and crass—no disrespect. You don't have to even Talk to the bitch. Give her the dough and walk her to the motel door or kick her out, depending on her performance. Don't see her again. No need to. Go for a new one, if you so choose.

You tell the service that you want a caucasian or sultry choc-olate brown(not pitch black) twenty-something brunette or blonde, athletic, slender with a 34B natural (No fake tits) GFE (girlfriend experience, meaning a girlfriend in good times) Then you shower, get squeaky clean, soap your erogenous zone twice, take your Viagra pill (take one, don't give me that "oh, I don't need that" you do, it turbocharges the system, she will be thankful,) look in the mirror, give yourself a high five and congratulate yourself. After showering, look yourself in the mir-ror again, grin and say, "Oh, you handsome devil, don't you ever die."

An hour later there is a soft knock on the door. You have butterflies in your stomach, dying with mystery and anticipation.

The notion of payment for sex is alien and repugnant to many. Purists condemn it, while engaging in it themselves. The names of hypocritical ministers, priests, bishops and other clergy would fill pages. Public figures, including the governors of South Carolina, California, and New York were caught red-handed and now the President of France is caught chasing an actress on a scooter. What's up with these Frenchmen?

The downside of engaging in this activity is that one has to deal with the dark underbelly of society where drugs, disease, and violence is rampant. Whether our moral or ethical values accept or reject the business of prostitution, the fact is that it is as old as humankind. It may be a necessary evil.

Bartering, trading goods and services with each other, is as old and as natural as recorded history. There is nothing sinister about it. Some transactions are transparent, others less defined or vague. Some have an implied objective and others, a clear one. I have seen the underbelly of society, and it is not pretty. From viewing pornography to visiting striptease bars and adult stores, I have traveled the whole circuit throughout the Americas. I have participated in Skin trade with excitement, fear, and fascination.

Nirvana is a state of freedom from all suffering. Buddhists believe it can be achieved by renouncing worldly possessions and desire. Bull? Severe body pain exists, along with morbid thoughts!

Life is not a bed of roses all the time; it is painful, both physically and emotionally. A smart, well-informed and conscientious person can minimize the pain and suffering, but not eliminate it. One should guard against living in a bubble or developing a tunnel vision. It is even worse if one is simply in a denial. When I am wrong, I quickly admit it. It's good to let go of the ego and false pride.

In his short masterpiece *As a man Thinketh*, James Allen wisely compares the mind to a garden—a beautiful analogy. Allen says that if you don't cultivate your garden, plant the right seeds, cut the waste and harmful weeds and keep the mind garden well-tended, plants will wilt and die and wild plants will take over. You will no longer have a beautiful garden. A beautiful mind needs to be 'planted,' with the right thoughts, nurture them and replace any bad or ugly thoughts with good ones.

Sweeping facts under the rug won't work. It's downright stupid. Apologizing does not diminish us in any way. An apology elevates us. It builds character and strengthens us. We must accord respect to people, animals, and even things. It may help in relating to others. We all are sometimes weak, envious and susceptible to making mistakes. Only God is perfect, right? Am I boring you, should you rather talk about sex...

Living with often excruciating pain on a daily basis is becoming unbearable. The mental fog caused by taking heavy doses of medicine regularly is awful. My body has not been the same since the damn doctors fused the spine with titanium plates. I am physically struck by all kinds of maladies. The constant and severe bowel and bladder problems have been hellish.

To live with joy and dignity has been a challenge, to say the least. It is difficult to pay attention to everyday life when the rectum is exploding like a volcano with an imaginary lava pouring out, crying out for mercy. It takes all my might and patience to smile with sincerity. Patience, my ass. I feel like I want to kill somebody, a doctor? How many of you want to kill the 'other' lawyer or your ex-spouse?

Ever dance alone in the rain? Did you know that when you are dancing you are never unhappy, unless you are a Natalie Portman in **Black Swan**. Ever see scowling faces on the dance floor? Find me someone who doesn't like music, children, sunsets or sex, and I will show you an ass wipe.

During the first few months, maybe even the first few years, after my near fatal injury, I was numb with pain. The uncertainty and the reality of living the rest of my life within the confines of a wheelchair were chilling. I was shell-shocked by the cata-strophic incident. Gradually I acquired calmness of mind and some humor to accept this as a humbling shakedown by powers-that-be. I was living too good of a life.

I was suddenly shy; My heart moved through silent but deep waters. Nothing and no one interested me or made me very happy. I remained tough, but confused, a sad and tragic state to be in. I wanted to to be a good example to my children, who were grown up now. It broke their hearts to see their father in such horrific state. I reminded myself that it is not what happens to you, it is how you respond to it, how you deal with it, that must be the true measure of a man or a woman.

A couple of years after the incident, I had the great pleasure of a visit from Goodman. We had hung out, played and worked together in the 1980s. Goodman and I had started my business together if you been paying attention. Goodman went on to fly a DC-6 for an air cargo outfit in Alaska for the next decade-plus. Then he worked for a quasi-government operation, flying in the troubled region of the Southern Philippines where the Muslim South is fighting an insurgency against the Christian north. The damn Muslims always want to fight. They are on a mission to Convert the infidel, like the Christian missionaries. Many will kill you if you are a Kafir (an unbeliever.)

Goodman and I once were inseparable and did many good and bad things together in our late twenties. He is a fascinating man who has my attention. In the late eighties, we had a fall-ing out over few issues. He left the States in the early nineties. This incredible man with a large heart and a loving Thai spouse bought a sailboat and sailed around the world for a decade. Being a world traveler and a renaissance man, he has led a remarkable life and has many interesting tales to tell.

We had a few beers one night recently and reminisced about old times, remembering the joys and sorrows of years gone by. With age one loses memory but gains insight. What struck me as odd was, how my version of the issues that led to our breakup in the eighties was Vastly different from his. Surprised? When we let our guard down. No one is immune. I keep that insight in mind and fight the loser tendency to point fingers and see others at fault without introspection on my part first. Goodman and I both thought that the other was at fault. Things are Not always as we see, feel, hear or understand, especially when emotions get involved. Our five senses are notoriously unreliable. The only reliable sense is the sixth sense, the sense of humor... really! The morbid thoughts and severe pain linger.

Our good friend from Alaska, MM got into the construction business, building homes. He seemed happy, content and in love when I visited him in 2003. I was quite impressed with MM's simple life. No stress? In 2007, his beloved wife died of unknown causes. Excessive alcohol and tobacco use may have contributed to her death. MM was devastated. He flew to Hawaii where they had been married. He scattered her ashes in the Pacific, according to her wishes. My heart went out to him.

The transience of life, coupled with the uncertainty of the moment, is the greatest mystery of all. You never know what will happen tomorrow or even in the next minute. Life ought to be lived as we stand Now. Not tomorrow, not next week or next month, but right now, with no regrets and with no wishes or desires unmet.

I ask myself: Am I a finished product as I am? Am I one with myself, my family, my real friends and my circumstances? Am I meeting my obligations satisfactorily and with dignity? If not, then one is probably in trouble. Waste no time; get your lazy ass off the mental couch, lose the remote and start working on being happy Now. Rearrange the furniture of your mind. Question the basic assumptions of your being. Lose your druggie boyfriend or the gold digger chick friend. Get a better job, open a business—whatever the hell it takes, get it done. It can be done.

Being disabled and totally at the mercy and goodwill of others changes your worldview a little, to say the least. Throw in a shitty hemorrhoid condition, it is no laughing matter. It is a royal pain in the ass. Most people look forward to taking a dump. I dread it. Pile up excruciating pain on top of it and you have a perfect (shitty) storm. A better man would say that the only disability one has is that of a bad attitude.

I am quite cynical about modern medicine. Eastern cures seem hokey. There are many paths to pursuing personal enlightenment. I am skeptical and somewhat weary of new age cures, like a primal scream, sensory deprivation, TM and so on. Same damn old message in a new package tied with ribbon and a bowtie. Ask Swami Deepak Chopra, he will give you the same message (and charge you 10k, or $100k depending on who you were.)

I am willing to try Anything to alleviate pain, even accepting Jesus Christ as my savior. Well, let's not go that far. Won't happen. Living with pain on a consistent basis; Priorities and expectations change or rearrange themselves. You find new sources of pleasure, like a good meal, chat with your daughter, a favorable conclusion to a business deal or the repair of broken relationships, especially those involving adversaries.

Talk about enemies or ill-wishers. The first thing I did when I was discharged from the hospital was to call a few of my known nemeses, maybe two or three, and ask to be forgiven for any harm or pain I may have caused them. I sincerely tried to make amends with everyone.

I read this note by Anonymous, "One day someone is going to hug you so tight that all of your broken pieces will stick back together." Hmm, interesting.

18

PROGRESS

Life is a work in progress; pursuit of excellence is always my goal, along with actions to better my circumstances and do my best to treat others well. Sometimes, one's best is not good enough. I rise early, seven days a week, saddle up with the help of a caregiver and go to work. Talk about caregivers, they are in a class of their own. Since the injury in April 2006, I think I have had five caregivers. The average shelf life of a caregiver has been six months to a year.

One of them, a woman named Angelica whom I liked, stole $4,400 in cash from me. The incident taught me not to leave too much cash lying around to tempt other's integrity. I am dependent on caregivers. I would rather be alone but can't; someone is with me most of the time. I am told that I am the source of strength and inspiration to those who know me. Many people have told me what a great example I am setting by not giving up. I wish they wouldn't do that. It's not easy being me... lol. It has been 9 years since I was injured. I am almost getting used to my limited lifestyle options.

The quintessential American hero and my old pal, Boslo, and I spoke after almost a decade one night. We discussed some precious memories from what seems like centuries ago. God, how I loved that man. Like most of our friends in our age group, his hearing has gone south. Email and texting are the keys to communication. He is busy raising his relatively large family and tending to his thriving business in Anchorage. He owns a couple of cabins in the bush and has two airplanes that take him to his hideouts in parts of Alaska that are accessible only by air. He seems happy, optimistic and prosperous. Good for him. You go, Boslo, my own CNN hero!

Morbid thoughts persist. Do I want to End it all? I find myself checking the Amtrak schedule fast train when a fast train goes by, There is something about millions of pounds of steel barreling down the track at sixty or seventy miles per hour. It's 3:33 p.m. At times I often feel like taking it on, looking straight into the motherfucker at seventy miles per hour.

SJ is another business buddy who slowly became a friend. He is a very successful airplane dealer, another icon of general aviation who has done business with me for over two decades. I look up to him for his incredible knowledge, resources, and counsel. He is a very interesting, shrewd and honest professional, married to a rich, forty-something, compatible and beautiful woman who has a sunny disposition and undying loyalty. Now, I am good at plane sales, but SJ is a true wizard. He's unbelievable with numbers, has total memory recall and carries his balls in a wheelbarrow. They lived in northern California, but due to his distaste for the state of California and his love of the wilderness, flying, fishing and hunting, they moved to Alaska.

SJ is an enigma. He ordinarily exercises good common sense, but when he deals with authorities, his senses take a leave of absence. My good buddy becomes angry, bitter and resentful of the way he perceives our country is being run, especially by the present administration. He thinks that Government is out to fuck him. It sure Doesn't help to have a Brother in the white house. His right-wing attitude and flawed understanding of the affairs of the government have recently gotten him in trouble with the law. He thumbed his nose at the authorities, so they pulled a sting on him. They threw the book at him for a few violations that most people would ordinarily get away with.

One should never take on the Man with a gun And the badge; that is the equivalent of taking on the great might of the U.S.A.

SJ sold several aircraft to Mexicans and did not personally report the cash transactions to the government as required by law. The law mandates that any transaction over $10,000 in Cash must be reported by filing a cash transaction report (CTR) with Customs. JS allegedly failed to do so. He says that was because the buyers directly deposited the cash into his bank account, thus absolving him of the CTR requirement. I thought so too that it has to be a banker's job not the account holder's.

His company has been charged with money laundering. The many deposits just under $10,000 showed a pattern of skirting the law. SJ faces probation and huge fines and legal fees to the tune of one million dollars. This unfortunate episode has angered him further, eroding his already bruised confidence in our system, which he sees as corrupt and out to get the rich and redistribute wealth to the poor. Instead of being thankful for our system that provides conditions to thrive, people bitch and flip the bird. Result; lives of discontent, feeling of helplessness. Money becomes the metric of success.

SJ is becoming a recluse, spending time in the wilderness of Alaska. Due of his smarts, wealth and lack of humility, SJ has made few enemies in the aviation industry, most of whom are just plain jealous. I truly admire him; he's my own CNN hero. We talk, shoot the breeze, buy and sell airplanes regularly. He is one of the most trustworthy, straightforward and honorable fellows I have ever known, a man of impeccable credentials and integrity.

He is an unfortunate victim of his own thought patterns, impenetrable, unbending and stuck in his ways. Sad, but true.

Have you ever said *if I had a million dollars I would be the happiest person in the world?* Having money would help you attain material comforts and give you a sense of security that you do not have now. However, there are things in life that no amount of money can buy e.g. peace of mind, true friends, love, health, happiness and emotional fulfillment.

A little detour, a sad one, a tragic loss. My dearest brother and friend TG died. He died of leukemia two months after he was diagnosed with the disease. He passed away in a hospital in Karachi. He was the first sibling of the eleven of us to die. He leaves behind a son, Harry, eighteen years old. Harry is a very loving and bright young man.

TG and I were best buddies growing up. We were opposites, yet very close. He was better looking, fairer and more talented than I was back then. He sang, danced, told jokes, the life of the party. His sense of humor, cutting wit and cynicism are legendary. I was his sidekick. TG never drank, smoked pot or did any drugs. He was a straight arrow and a bit ignorant. He had religious leanings similar to most of our family members. TG and I loved each other but had sibling rivalry, jealous of each other when we were young. We were forever competing but together.

One time in our teens, I liked a girl and she was fond of me. I told my brother about this hot chick I was having a tryst with. He said he wanted to meet her. I agreed, but warned him, "Don't mess with her and muddy up my deal." TG looked at me and replied, "Of course not, my Prince. Why would I do that for?" **We called each other 'prince.'**

I introduced him to her, a huge mistake. He started flirting with her, and she fell for this better version of me. I was filled with romantic angst and teenage jealousy. He sang to her and charmed her with his romantic wit, poetic expressions, and a better hairdo that he was proud of. I protested. He dismissed me,

"Prince, she is mine now and there is nothing you can do about it." Cocksucker.

That was devastating to this tortured Romeo. It injured my raw feelings and a strong ego immensely. I was emotionally wounded by the betrayal of two people, I loved. TG had an affair with her for many years, finally dumping her for another girl. I was wickedly happy, thinking she deserved it. However, I wanted to get even with my brother.

My good looking brother loved his hairdo.

Our parents had put us in a boarding school to discipline us. TG and I shared a room. I carried the grudge and wanted to strike back at him for his betrayal. I was also jealous of his better looks, especially his hairdo. One night, I woke around midnight while he slept, grabbed the sharp scissors I had hidden under my pillow.

I went over to his bed where he was sound asleep, snoring. I grabbed a clump of hair on the front of his head, and with one jealous swipe, I cut his cherished hairdo. He woke up immediately and realized what had happened. He was the angriest that I had ever seen him. He slapped me hard and ran from the room. Had he been stronger, he would have whipped my ass, but too bad. I was stronger, I felt justified because he had taken my girl away from me.

TG wanted to be an actor, but he never could make the grade. After I left abroad in 1975, he stayed behind and sort of withered away, not succeeding in any line of work he chose. He wanted to work in the music, film, and entertainment world. He always carried a video recorder with him, filming every fucking thing. He was addicted to his camera, and we all had to comply with his requests to be filmed.

In late Nineties, he called me from Karachi, saying that he was broke and wanted to move to the United States. TG reminded me that I owed it to him to help him. That's what family members are supposed to do. The more fortunate should help the ones who lag behind, to pull themselves up by their bootstraps, regardless of merit. He had a point. So I helped him get his immigration status by sponsoring him.

On his arrival in California, I gave him $10,000 cash plus bought him a new car with my cold cash. I felt indebted, compassionate and wanted to help my blood. Incidentally I also helped RG, my hard-working younger brother, get his citizenship. That is a story and a half in itself. I better leave RG alone. You don't want to stir the hornist's nest. RG was nicknamed 'Dainboo,' meaning hornet.

I thought that, like me, TG would work hard and make a future for himself. Boy was I wrong. Instead, he turned out to be a lazy bum, spending his time videotaping, watching TV, shopping, sightseeing and napping. He did some dead-end jobs but didn't succeed at anything. He had his hand out and was always hitting me up for money. One time my brother pulled a fast one on me that shocked me.

It was no secret that I was playing around, I didn't want my wife to know. I had kept $55,000 'play money' in a bank account in my brother's name with me as an additional signatory. We had, of course, agreed that it's my money, he won't touch my money.

I often took my family on Mexican Riviera 7-day cruises. On this one trip, when we returned, I checked with the bank. My $55,000 were gone. I was dumbfounded. My trusted brother TG, with the connivance of RG, had withdrawn the cash and closed the account.

Now what? He had betrayed my trust again. I was both furious and disappointed in my blood. I didn't know how to get my money back. Think like Machiavelli.

I went to Los Angeles, where he lived with his wife and son. First, I asked him nicely to return my money, which, as expected, he refused to do. Then I threatened to call the police. I scared him by saying that, not only would I call the police, I also would hire goons (who work on a percentage basis. I assured him.) They would beat him up, break his son's legs and take my money from him by force. He wouldn't budge. Bad bluff? Then I tricked him;

I became nice and let the honey attract the bees. "Prince what are you going to Do with the money?" I think he was listening.

After I had got his attention, I hid my fury and faked compassion, "What were you going to do with the money, Prince?" He reluctantly and sheepishly replied, "Prince, I want to buy a seven-eleven [store], and I will return your money once I make money." I thought, you mother…that will never happen. Bad idea. I bluffed him and told him that a 7-Eleven store would cost $250,000, not $55,000. I put my arm around his small shoulders and feigned affection, while reality was I wanted to kill him, 'My prince why didn't you tell me that.' He looked at me with suspicion. I lied, "Well prince I would help you buy 7/11 and maybe you all family members can run it. I will be a silent partner. I can save on taxes." I held my breath.

We have four nephews who live in the city of angels including his son.

I think he believed me, he looked at RG, who may have nodded in agreement. After some sweet talk back and forth, he lovingly said, "Prince, you are known as a man of your word, don't disappoint us. Do buy us the store." TG then hesitatingly wrote me a check for $50,000. He had already spent a little over $5,000 on trinkets, like electronics, clothing and VCR, etc. I was relieved. I found a willing Bank of America (BOA) official and deposited about $1,200 in the account so that I could cash the $50,000 check at BOA. The account had depleted to $48,800. Any deal signed under duress is illegal.

After that incident, I cut him off and did not talk to him for a couple of years. I was so hurt by my brother, whom I had helped to get the much coveted American citizenship, bought him a new car and gave him ten grand in cash. I never trusted him again. After a lackluster stay in L.A., TG despaired and went back to Pakistan, thinking he would try his luck there. He was unhappy, a bit depressed and always behind the curve. He desperately wanted to make money. He got a cushy job in Karachi through connections. He called me three years later, asking for help - again. After two years of estrangement, I was moved with sympathy for my brother in need, so I said, "Okay, Prince, come back to the States; I will help you," and I meant it. "Let me know and I'll buy you an airline ticket."

Week later TG was admitted to the hospital with severe stomach pain in December 2011. A biopsy followed, and he was diagnosed with leukemia, which led to blood transfusions at regular intervals. After a painful struggle, he passed away and was buried immediately with no embalming, which is the Muslim tradition.

I lost a good friend and a dear brother. He was a simple man, but left an indelible good impression on all of us, except RG, who hated his guts till the end. He left behind a son who must have been lost and devastated. TG took the poor kid to Pakistan, kicking and screaming, when my nephew was barely fifteen. I like Harry. Maybe I am destined to play a role in my nephew's life someday. I told TG I would. Should anyone take revenge? No. Sons must never be visited upon by the sins of their fathers. Reality is the opposite. Most Pakis take revenge from the sons and their sons for generations.

What good is anger or resentment or a wish to avenge a wrong and exact justice? It is like a monkey on your back; it will pull you down. Let the makers dispense justice. Hatred is bad in any form, even when fully justified. Hatred is hatred. Revenge, too, is in a similar category. Kick ass if you have to, don't hate, forgive.

Who are we to exact justice anyway? People are so full of themselves, thinking that they are the masters of the universe and that they can arbitrarily shape the world and change the course of life so that events will bend to favor them. It's foolish and arrogant. Let the gods deal with such inequities and miscarriages of justice. We do not decide who lives and who dies. Who knows why shit happens or does not happen? All I know and see is that, with few exceptions, you get what you deserve right here on earth. Hell and heaven exist on earth. You make your bed and you sleep in it.

It is best to move on. Make peace, forgive and forget. I try to be detached, dispassionate and fact-centered. I control my emotions by stopping the shitty sentimental thoughts the moment they pop into my head so that I don't get carried away with emotion. You can do it, I swear. I did it and I'm not any better than or any different from you. Did I get from life what I deserve? Maybe, maybe not. I will never know.

One fact is obvious: If you decide to live in today's universe, you must accept that there is violence in the world, that shit happens and that rulers and rules change. Home invasions occur. People get shot; they die in car, plane or train accidents—hell—even on bicycles. You cannot stop any of it. Don't even bother. Leave it to powers bigger than we are. Karma will catch up, eventually.

I hope that my daughters, too, will get closure and move on. This reminds me that this memoir would be incomplete without mentioning the most important people in my life, my two lovely girls and my muse, my friend and companion, my benefactor and tormentor—for better or worse—my Ex.

19

MY DAUGHTERS

I write about them at my own peril and pleasure. Hey, as I said, everyone is someone's daughter, just as precious or just as rotten. I got married for one reason only: to be a father, to have children and raise them as responsible, happy and honorable citizens, perpetuating all that is good in this world. That was the challenge I wanted to take on. Despite my difficult marriage, I stayed the course and did not divorce until they were sufficiently grown and able to carry their own loads, as adults. That was my covenant. Remember, I try to follow thru with my word. They are still in their formative years and the result so far has been a mixed bag.

I indulged them longer than customs or traditions required. I wanted them to live with us for as long as they wanted. I knew it meant that I would have to take care of them way longer than most parents do. I knowingly took on their financial dependence.

I didn't think there was any harm in helping them out for a little longer. I read something interesting about the animal kingdom, a fascinating tale; The dangerous and powerful mama grizzly ferociously guards and protects her cubs until they are grown, and only mama grizzly knows when they are ready to be on their own. One fine day, mama grizzly looks her cubs over, licks them gently, then turns around and leaves, never to see them again.

My girls are complete opposites. Both are smart, beautiful and the 'Apples of my eye' the dearest things to me in all creation. I have been very close to them all their lives. The very sight of them, even the thought of them, their voices, their presence, makes me smile and fills me with joy. Most of my life choices have been made with their well-being in mind. Isn't that the way a good father is supposed to be?

Thoughts of ending it all are always present. The freaking pain in the ass takes me back to the train tracks. I looked at the time on my iPhone, 7:30 p.m. Amtrak passes at 7:33 p.m.

When I decided to move out of Alaska to a warmer climate, one of my projects was to research the location. If you live in a nice neighborhood, then the issue of schooling is a done deal for me. Good neighborhoods have good schools. Private schools are overblown. It spawns more divisions than unions. I wanted to always live close to my little girls who soon wouldn't be little anymore.

I didn't care to send them to the Harvards and Stanfords of the world as I don't believe in private or prestigious schooling. I don't think the price you pay for them is worth the return. Each to their own. I went to bad schools and lived in rough neighborhoods and I turned out ok or did I? I think what really matters is creating a nice environment and love at home.

I have a theory on basic relationships of any kind...

If one spends many years in any skilled field, it will consume all your time. Having only twenty-four hours in a day, if one spends many hours at schooling, you will not be left with enough time to eat, sleep, fuck or forge relationships. One may acquire many degrees and have money to throw at things, but precious friends and family members require time. You won't have enough time to lovingly listen, ask relevant questions and participate in their lives. The downside of getting degrees in one's chosen fields of endeavor is that one may be left with fewer true friends or caring family members.

One probably will end up being lonely, as you may come off as being rude, aloof and uninterested in fellow beings. I know doctors, lawyers and big business owners who have trouble in social settings and have superficial, awkward relationships. They lack genuine friends and generally in trouble with their children. Doctors reportedly have the highest suicide rates in America. Back to Sheila and Geena…

I thought If they went far away to school, I would lose the four precious years during which they would be away at college growing up without really interacting with me. Then when they graduated, they would be in high demand and would end up wherever the best career opportunities took them. I would rarely see them, which was not acceptable to me. I do not believe in high living, I think simplicity is good for human beings. Guaranteed!

The stress involved in making it big cannot be good for you. Having a lot of money generally results in having a lot of stress. I know that firsthand. I had a lot of money once, but, man, I had a lot of problems too. When you have a lot of cash, everybody, and their dog wants some of your money. Strangers, friends, relatives all want to borrow, steal, sue, you name it.

I never cared for Disneyland, Sea world, Magic Mountain or Safari Park. I do not like to see animals in cages and aquariums or behind walls and barbed wire fences. For that reason, I don't like dogs, cats and other animals, like lizards and snakes, as animals belong in the wild, not in peoples' homes; they are not meant to entertain humans. It offends my sense of fairness to see people around the globe, especially those in the affluent west, acquiring animals for entertainment, friendship. Oh, Nigga please, cultivate human friendships. It's hard work but very rewarding.

I have a special contempt for those who raise dogs and some other animals to fight. That seems barbaric. It is one thing to raise your child with a puppy, but it is wrong to raise an animal to fight. Affluent Pakis love watching animals fight each other to barbaric death. Animals like chickens, dogs vs. bears, snake vs. mongoose, etc.

The toughest battles I had with my girls were about pets. Like any other children in the West- not East-they wanted a puppy. I refused. They would beg and beg me for one, and I would say no and No. Finally, I relented on the condition that we would 'try out' a Yorkshire Terrier for few weeks. After that, if I couldn't cohabit, the dog would have to go. They innocently agreed, perhaps not knowing what a promise or contract meant.

After the few weeks were up, I told them that the experiment was over. I could not bear to have an animal in my living quarters. The barking, the smell, the hair. The girls cried, screamed and pled with me, "Oh, Papa, please, please." I couldn't talk them into getting rid of the dog.

You are going to hate me for this and I don't care. I called my nephews in L.A. and asked them for help. They agreed to come and pick up the Yorkshire puppy that the girls had named, Riley. I told my nephews to sell the dog and keep the money. They gladly agreed. One day, when the girls were out of the house, I rang up the nephews and gave 'em the green light. It was quite a scene watching four or five of my family, running after that little ball of energy, Riley, who perhaps knew of the plan and ran from them. Quite a circus. Do animals know, but can't do anything about it?

Well, the rest is history. When the girls returned, they looked for Riley, and of course, there was no Riley. I was the main suspect, but as planned, I denied knowing anything about the missing dog. This happened in our household a few times. I allowed a dog, swayed by the girls' pressure. Then I made a dog, rabbit, bird, and the cat disappear.

Damn pain and burning persist. Bastard won't go away! Now you are all saying, "Good. Suffer, you dog." I understand. I concur.

Despite my marital difficulties, I was determined to remain married as I did not want my girls to grow up in a broken home. I did ask myself whether growing up in a warring home is better than in a divorced? Hell, I got married in the first place to have children. I went to Lamaze classes with my pregnant wife. I was with her when she gave birth to both girls in an Anchorage hospital. Watching my first born, Sheila, emerge from mother's womb and cutting the umbilical cord was a totally surreal and rapturous moment. It was simply awesome. I wish that experience upon all willing fathers. It caused a tectonic shift to my psyche, for the better.

I was a changed man that night. I cried uncontrollably. I fell in love with that sweet, cuddly baby. I vowed to be a good parent to her and not get into any trouble that would jeopardize my freedom and prevent me from seeing her every day of my life. I bought sweets and pastries from the bakery and distributed them among patrons of the dance club I usually frequented. They seemed a bit surprised at the offerings and gave me weird looks. Distributing sweets is a tradition in Pakistan, a tradition I had retained and there are many good traditions, strengths of that culture. It is the bad ones that I rejected.

I was determined to be a good father. I changed diapers, which Paki dads don't, played with Sheila and made sure that her mother could be a stay-at-home mom so that she could care for our daughter full time. make it happened I worked 18 hours a day in freezing temperatures, shoveling snow from a row of small planes I owned or had 'em consigned. Sheila was a slice of heaven, caring, congenial, beautiful, driven and self-sufficient. She was almost a model child growing up, never getting into any trouble and getting good grades in school. She is sociable, loved by everyone and very thoughtful of us all.

Sheila is classy, not classy in mere wealth, lineage or attitude, but in integrity, compassion and courage. She was the best child that any parent could ask for. Both my daughters initially went to college in Santa Barbara, took a year off when I got hurt, so they could be with me day and night. I am forever thankful for that.

Sheila graduated from a college in San Francisco, making us proud. After graduation, Sheila and her roommate, Tiff, went on a vacation to Bali with a stopover in Thailand, they never made it. Both girls met two vacationing men, an Irishman and an Australian on a scenic island. They both fell in love. After a year or two of a long distance relationship, pining for her boyfriend, Sheila moved to Australia to be with him. Her roommate, Tiff, went a step further and married the Irishman and moved to London. How is that for a couple of love stories?

Now Sheila lives a fairy tale life in the tropical part of Northeast Australia with this remarkable Aussie man of Lebanese descent. They are truly in love. Sheila has been gone for some time, and her absence gnaws at me, her mother and her sissy.

Geena, my younger daughter, is in a class by herself. She is a very precious, precocious and a clever girl, with a good heart, means well but has struggled overcoming drugs. Geena is sweet, gregarious and a fashionable girl. She is a flower child, a throwback to the hippie movement. She is the darling of all her friends and family. I have an eternal deep umbilical connection with her. Due to her lifestyle choices, future may not bode well for her.

Geena has a propensity to get into trouble and disregard the rules. She kept questionable company and took up partying, clubbing, doing drugs and drinking at an early age. I loved Geena to no end, perhaps ennobling her? I spoiled her with lavish things. I was not the stern father I should have been. I failed to keep my eye on the ball, did not pay attention and let her slip...She has become lazy. She is very unusual and one of a kind.

Geena is a sensitive and thoughtful person, devoid of jealousy and anger. She does not take care of her body and mind. She is irreligious, rebellious and a nonconformist, irreverent of tradition. She is independent, free-spirited and easy-going, with a love of laughter, joy, and dance. Geena is wild, wondrous, but wanders, always walking on the edge, a master manipulator, who endears herself to anyone her heart desires. She is loved and desired by many and dissed by few.

She dropped out of college and lives with us, but disappears for days, even weeks, and does not communicate with us despite our pleas. I am distressed by her lifestyle and her inattention to things that really matter in life, like family and a career. Those who know me say that she is like me, that she has my troublesome genes. Upon learning of my gunshot, she overcame by shock and grief, fainted and stayed lost for a while. I was larger than life for her. Never in the history of a father-daughter relationship, has the father-daughter adored and loved each other, as much as the two of us until the gunshot.

I delegated their upbringing to her mother, a Paki tradition. I tried to be fair and just. I didn't ground the girls, punish them or deny them any privileges. I wanted them to be free, strong and happy. I did not want them to grow up feeling that I was unreasonable, autocratic and strict, curtailing their liberties just because I could. I fought with my ex-wife constantly, telling her to let them be children and let them play. Terrible pain persists. Are the gods punishing me?

My girls put their lives on hold and dropped out of college to be with me back in 2006. The hospital staffs at ICU and Rehab were impressed with their 24/7 watch on their old man. Geena crawled into bed and lay beside me all the time to keep my cold, shivering body warm. Sheila was the smart one in the family who calmly took control of the finances, logistics and guided my recovery with a calm, cool, steady hand.

My ex attended to my every need around the clock, bringing me home-cooked meals, bathing me, massaging me, keeping the doctors and the nurses in line—working overtime. She cleaned me, kept me entertained and wouldn't let me die. My family made me aware of how lucky I was to have my family. They were by the hospital bedside, there for me for the better part of the year. The three of them took turns and helped me, make a speedier recovery.

Maybe it was time for them to move on. After all, they are adults and had to do what a girl has to do. Sheila is very close to her mother. They are soul mates. Her mother, while foolishly supporting her move across the world, probably pines for Sheila and sobs in her sleep, missing our daughter. She loves Sheila immeasurably.

Sheila is an athletic chick with clear brown eyes and glistening skin. She is the one with the brains, well mannered, elegant and articulate with a sunny disposition. She is so beautiful, she would give a dead man a hard-on ... Smiles!

Sheila has a secure sense of self, modern in thought, modest, fashionable in attire and taste, full of vigor, optimism and a zest for life. She is a creature like me, with similar interests and values, open minded and happy. She loves to play, dance, surf, and socialize, along with seriously reflecting on how to live an honorable and good life. She works hard and plays hard. It must not be easy being around, a hard-drinking, hard-working Aussie group made up of serious partiers, but sober executives. Aussies are generally sweet and likable.

Damn it, I tell her to find a way to be in the States with us. Bring him with you; use your beauty, charm, logic and intellect to persuade him that he can come too. If he truly loved you, he would respect your wish to be close to your family, unless he felt that it wasn't that important to you. Unless he felt that you were so intoxicated by love that you wouldn't push. I would be the last person to encourage any break up of two loving hearts.

Geena is my baby, but a spoiled one, a brat whom I have indulged too much, too long, like buying her a Lexus on her sixteenth birthday. She is irresponsible and sort of unaware of the consequences of her actions and their possible effect on her future. Unless she makes a turnaround soon, she will have a tough life. You can't mess around with hard drugs. Being a father, I worry. She thinks she can overcome all hurdles and lives in oblivion regarding the future consequences. I could stop supporting her, but her mother won't allow it. She nurtures Geena to death and probably holds herself responsible for Geena's wayward ways.

The tricky daughter has her mommy wrapped around her pinky finger. When Geena says jump, her mother asks how high. I have never seen two women, who have such a loving, but odd, confrontational relationship. Mom and daughter fight like cats, driving me nuts, I swear.

Some time ago thoughts of the futility of life kept recurring. I couldn't seem to shake them off. For one, it is not that easy for a handicapped man to end it. I can't pull the fucking trigger as my fingers don't work, and I do not own a gun, can't hang myself. I can't drive off a cliff as I don't drive. I have read that overdosing on pills is not a sure thing as they can pump the shit out of your stomach, and then you are more damaged than before. Train tracks? Hmm…like to, but it would be messy, pieces of damn flesh everywhere on the tracks. Girls won't dig that. Wicked smiles!

I am very mindful of leaving two devastated daughters behind if I were to go for the nuclear option. Despite their apparent absence, I am quite sure they will be back in my life and spend more quality time with their old man. Try to make lemonade out of lemons? Well, I could, If I had my girls by my side, rooting for me to go on and talking with me regularly. They know how so immensely, I am fond of them, and that I have a difficult spousal relationship, which brings me to the crux of the issue. The critical factor? My relationship with my ex, once my master caregiver.

On the advice of my doctor, I went to see a shrink early in 2012. First time ever.

While in the ICU, a shrink, a priest and a young starry-eyed christian singer with a guitar were my regular visitors. Perhaps they were on the hospital's payroll, but the only one I paid attention to was the sexy chick who sang hymns, I was still in 'skirt-chasing' mode. The guitar playing chick seemed to have found her Nirvana, i.e., Jesus. The shrink found me boring and, on cue, didn't come around much. It was quite interesting to see how the hospital, with its huge grants from donors, subtly bent its secular rules to Christianize the ill and the dying in the ICU. Good trick, but it won't work on me, a KAFIR.

For me, it was a bit creepy to see a damn priest in my ward. I was too drugged to yell at him to get out and take the god dang psychologist with him. Just leave the sexy chick to keep singing me the lullabies. I remember my first few days in the ICU, breaking down a couple of times and weeping like a baby in random nurse's arms, wishing I were dead and asking for more morphine to dull the hellish pain. Every few nights a peculiar bell would sound in the ICU, signaling a patient's grave condition so that the appropriate staff would be notified when a death occurred. One night when that peculiar bell rang, I thought I had died, and I saw my funeral preparations. It was surreal. "I wanted cremation, you fuckers," I screamed at the staff.

All my life, I thought that, since I was the maker, shaper and the chief architect of my life, I did not need anyone, any outsider, to tell me how to live my life. I was the Governor of my province, even when I misgoverned, I was still the Governor. I thought that to fix myself, all I had to do was to look inward and dig deep into the reservoir of inner strength to find solace, guidance, and solutions to the problems and issues. I thought I was the only one who had gotten me off track, and I was the one who could get me back. Who else would know me as good as I do?

Yes, like a President or a King, I need advisors to guide and navigate through the morass of governorship. Well, isn't that what real friends are for? You confide in friends and family and make them your allies. Give them the relevant information and freedom to speak their truth. Let them feel free to voice their opinions and give them a fair hearing. Get to know them well. Invest in your friends so that you can turn to them-not shrinks-for advice. When shit goes south, ask friends about the things that ail you.

Don't just share joys and laughter alone; sorrow is the other side of the coin. A shrink will take forever to get to know you and find your solutions. The shrink may care, but he or she is there to make money. The shrink's main concern is their pocketbook, not you. When you tell your trusted friends your secrets, you essentially buy them an insurance policy. They will be the beneficiaries of you confiding in them, against you ever hurting their interest as retaliation would be swift. "Only your friends know your secret, and only they can reveal it," Bob Marley sang.

My ex is opening a high-end boutique, which has been her dream forever. Good intention but bad location. She won't listen. Hope we are all wrong, for her sake.

Great news. My daughters are promising to come back into my life and give me a helping hand, and I am quite certain that, as long as I am a gentleman—fair and just—my ex will be there for me, also, she claims she is in love with me. I am the only man she has ever been with or even kissed. I believe it. I guess the pledge 'till death do us part' is still taken seriously by some. A velvet hand, but an iron fist? She is A terror to reckon with. I ought to be given an award for enduring her.

I am feeling great, spiritually, emotionally and mentally charged, but physical pain and discomfort are still a Motherfucker! I can't seem to whip this baby. I keep reminding myself that the will to endure pain builds character and teaches you a few things about patience, tolerance, and perseverance.

I need to think of myself as an MIG-19 or F-16, armed and dangerous, going after the Pain and destroying it. Blow the mofo to smithereens. Sometimes I think maybe the pain will go away gradually just like it came in. As I so eloquently stated earlier, it is a Mofo. But the pain doesn't know who it's dealing with; it doesn't know that I am not a quitter. I am a fighter, a fucking Roman gladiator, as you may agree by now.

Our five senses are incomplete without the sixth—a sense of humor. Just imagine if I had continued to live the way I was, as a master of the universe, the happiest man in the world? Imagine how cocky, unbearable and insolent I would have been (more than I am Now?) You would have seen a Donald Trump on steroids, a pompous bragger lacking any compassion or empathy. The tragedy would have been that I never would have known otherwise. Character traits like humility, consideration, compassion and kindness don't come easily. Some of us need them badly. I did.

Business has picked up again; I sold six airplanes in one month, a record month. I am starting to work longer hours and sleep better.

The other day I was embarrassed as I went to see an ass doctor, a proctologist. Now here is a job description for you to contemplate for the future: looking up assholes all day long. Yep, that's what he does—looks up the tunnel—bends you over on the table, puts on latex gloves, picks up an ass tool (yes, don't laugh, they make Ass tools), widens your hole and looks inside. One could get lost in that shitty Black Hole.

He looked up and happily said I had moderate inner hems and offered to remove them right there while his chick assistant had me bent over on the table. I hesitated for few seconds, not looking up keeping my face buried in the pillow, embarrassed. I buried my face deeper in the pillow and mumbled, "What are you waiting on Ass Doc, go for it."

Pain could be bladder related. I did have an operation sometime back, a suprapubic cystostomy. The urologist blocked off the normal urinary canal, rerouted the urinal passage and surgically inserted a catheter opening right above the pubic area, below the navel (the most erogenous area. Ah, sex!)

I carry a bag (into which I pee) attached to my leg. Well, look on the positive side; I don't have to be running to bathrooms to pee or have to get up in the middle of the night, to go to the bathroom (and get shot again...smiles.) It could be worse. I could be carrying a bag to poo. That operation is called a colostomy and is needed when, for a variety of reasons, the fecal exit has to be rerouted. Thank you, Allah, the merciful, for that minor distinction.

I just heard from my buddy MM, who was in the car accident in Grants Pass. In 1991 when we left Anchorage, we left our condo in MM's custody to find renters, manage. He rented it out to a deadbeat and did not collect rent for over a year, costing me thousands of dollars. I was chagrined at him. Oh well, I chalked it out to learning lessons and assume responsibility. I should have hired a property manager, not MM, who owned a travel agency.

MM told me that he had been convicted of third-degree assault with a deadly weapon, below vehicular manslaughter. Apparently he had been driving while heavily intoxicated. He smashed head-on into a pickup and put the other driver in the hospital with serious injuries. MM has a broken jaw and leg injuries. He pled guilty and got three years in the state prison.

MM was suffering from depression after his wife, Jacky, died of alcohol-related problems months earlier. MM is repentant and stoic about his fate. He is tying up loose ends in preparation for spending three years in an Oregon State prison. MM was the last guy anyone would have guessed, would be the kind of person who would end up going off his rocker. We all forget that the vehicle can be such a deadly weapon. How many of us think of that, when we sit behind the steering wheel, after drinking?

I thought MM lived a simple, but joyful, enviable life in a small town away from the hustle and bustle of the fast and furious life of the big cities. He had built a lovely house in rural Oregon, he was doing well and he was in love with his now-deceased wife. Oh well!

Doctors are puzzling to me. They generally make boring company and suffer from a godlike complex. The notion that they know best, you better listen—maybe because doctors meet people in their private domains, their small fiefdoms—or at hospitals or private clinics where their needy clients are helpless and looking for solutions or cures. Physicians are used to issuing orders and having us obey them. I wonder if the patient's anxiety and pain rub off on the doctors, making them miserable too.

20

ISLAM

Islam is said to be a controversial and
militant religion, full of kindness and unimaginable cruelty,
similar to Bible. It is also said to be a religion of peace,
but what good is the message of peace,
if won at the edge of the sword. Islam commands
Muslims to convert non-believers to Islam, first by peaceful
coercion. If they refuse, then... kill them. Ah kindness!
A Muslim converting to any religion is punishable by
death. Jews are dog meat in the Holy book. The cruelty is
such that just recently, TTP, a hardcore Muslim breakaway
terrorist organization sent six suicide bombers to attack
a military-run school, killing 141 people mostly children
of military personnel. A horrific Muslim record!
In my humble view Islam is designed for deaf, blind or mute,
suited for the poor, the lazy or someone with a gene mutation,
pre-disposed to faith. Stories of ancient kingdoms of enlightened
Muslims is irrelevant in Twenty-first century. Take this for a fact.
Nearly 180 million Pakis grow up reading Holy Quran, which is
written in Arabic, which no one understood, including me.

"Masses are asses," lamented Karl Marx, declaring to stunned readers, "Religion is the opiate of the people." He said. I think "Religion is a cosmic fraud invented by smart men—not women—centuries ago, to monopolize power and profit." You can quote me on that.

I thought that belief in faith partly stems from a fear of death, sense of superiority, the wish to be with your loved ones Again, and finally, the threat of retribution—hellfire. The lure and promise of a better afterlife with seventy virgins in heaven is attractive to those illiterates, whose lives on earth are barren and unbearable. I wonder if that is why Islamic countries spawn suicide bombers in droves, as the poor virgin bastards want to get the hell out of here and have sex with the promised virgins. Bible is equally horrific. A scholarly friend in Bible studies says,

Psalm 136 "O' daughter of Babylon, thou destroyer, blessed is he who shall repay thee the evils thou hast brought upon us! Blessed is he who shall seize and dash thy little ones against the rock" quoting direct from his grandmother's Catholic Bible. She came from Scotland. Nothing justifies such epic horror.

My lovely friend then talks to me "Oh my anguished friend, you are such a gift to mankind, don't stop talking." He feeds my ego. Gnawing n knifing and cruelty of unimaginable size is all over the Quran too. But do the believers backdown, no sir, the fools will double down on the lord.

By the afternoon, my only functioning middle finger refuses to write, giving comfort to Bible and Quran thumpers.

How could one believe in such providential nonsense? It's beyond me. Whereas men bombers get seventy virgins, the women bombers don't get shit. Surprisingly, they don't give a shit either. This is fit for *Ripley's Believe It or Not. T*his bizarre practice would make Robert Ripley shit.

We Can live a productive, peaceful life without all this bullshit. I know this first hand because I have lived it and raised two daughters without railroading them to submit to faith. Both are doing fine, thank you!

How could God Create individuals with the implicit upfront knowledge as to the fate and actions of each being? This question is the backbone of my argument. Why give people free will knowing fully well, that it will be used against Thou by nonbelievers? No one asks, not allowed to. Blasphemy!

The idea of heaven and hell is totally alien and surely fraudulent. Isn't earth your heaven or hell, depending on your deeds. Duh! You get what you deserve in this life - the only life we know of. I did, didn't you? If you live well, earth Is your heaven. If you are a douche bag, then you will be in hell right here. That simple.

Let me share some shameful commands of the Holy book with you, since Islam came 680 years after Christ.

The holy Quran mandates that it is incumbent on a Muslim parent to find a suitable man to marry his daughter right after she gets her first period. Each day the daughter stays under their roof after that will be a day of sin for them. Yes, it is hard to believe, but true. The holy book gives men authority over women, only addresses men, not women. Along with many good things, the holy books throw in some weird shit that is downright cruel, unusual, primitive and gender based. Machismo?

Here is another injustice: When a wife disobeys you, Quran commands you to whip her ass. If she continues to misbehave, take her out back and beat her harder and leave her there until she obeys you. Not many Muslims will say no to this favor by Allah. Beat the bitch with the baseball bat. The fucking morons get my blood boiling. Equality, what's that?

While we are at it, here is another mockery of jurisprudence: When you croak, Quran orders that three-quarters of the property shall go to your son and just one-quarter to your daughter. Muslim women never question it.

Women are given their due respect but considered second-class citizens under Islam. When I bring up such matters to Muslims, who dare discuss Islam with me, they start squirming and like President Clinton, they get lost in the meaning of the 'is' and then get raging mad.

The story of Prophet Abraham's absolute loyalty and obedience to Allah is beyond any horrible fiction. The tale is so inane, one might say, "Get the fuck out," but this is written in The Book that even diehard Muslims can't deny. Read on;

According to the holy Book, Allah wanted to test the obedience and devotion of Prophet Abraham. Allah, in a dream, ordered Abraham to prove his love and devotion. Abraham was ordered to sacrifice the most precious thing he had, his son. Now think a little, Wasn't there a better way for the Lord than to create a shit show. Give me a freaking break.

The Prophet took his son to a specific area as ordered. Just before Prophet Abraham was about to swipe the blade, there was divine intervention, an angel replaced the son with a sheep, lamb, goat or a ram. No one really knows.

'Honor killings' in the Islamic world are widespread, with men preying on servile women and helpless children. If Allah knew what was going to happen all along, then what was the point? Why did Allah ask Abraham to set a cruel and mindless precedence? Who would follow it? Only idiots.

Islam is big on dreams. It is comical, how shit happens to Muslims in their sleep. Prophet Muhammad also had revelations in a cave; he conversed with Angels in caves. Real angels, not Hell's Angels. Today, if someone claimed they had received such a revelation in a cave, they would be interned in a psychiatric institution.

Surely Allah knew of better ways to communicate with us. In Islam, if the shit is written in the Book, you don't question it. To question would be considered heresy, blasphemy, and a criminal act. Leave your damn inquiries at the door when you enter the mosque.

Carl Jung would have a field day interpreting these disturbing dreams of disturbed holy men.

Every year, Muslims—one billion of them, celebrate the festival of this barbaric sacrifice, by slaughtering an animal— even a damn camel. Depends on how much money you can afford. The idea behind this sacrifice is to have enough leftover meat (few Muslims are vegetarians) to distribute amongst the poor, the disenfranchised. And what really follows. Most meat is sent to friends, relatives, acquaintances.

Animals go apeshit in the days leading up to this day of goat fuck. During my childhood, every year I would go with dad to buy a scared shitless goat (Allah has probably whispered in the goat's ear, *you are fucked*) to be slaughtered the following day. Dad would hire a butcher to come to our house to kill a goat in a kosher manner. It's a violent comedy show. There is a stench of blood and death in the air.

The butcher wrestles the poor animal to the ground, slowly mumbling verses of the Quran while the goat goes berserk, squealing bloody murder with its feet kicking every which way. The butcher has a long knife with a sharp blade. He grabs the goat's throat and starts to slash, with blood squirting and splashing the butcher and anyone else within a six-foot radius. It's a comically grisly scene to witness. Ask any Muslim. He will verify it, *Prophet Abraham did it, so who the fuck am I not to? Try your newly born and then we will see.*

A lustful twist. In Islamic nations, marrying one's first cousin is preferred. Two of my brothers are married to distant cousins. One of my nephews is married to another of my niece. My brother Meesna frequently asked me to marry his son to my American-raised, liberal daughter, Geena, who recoiled in disgust and emphatically said, "NO."

Many Muslim first cousins fuck each other. I swear I am not making this up. They have been fucking each other for 1400 years, ever since Prophet Mohammad permitted it. Imagine the devastating results of fifty generations of inbreeding. According to a study by Nicolai Sennels, a renowned Danish professor, 70 percent of Pakis are doing each other and 50 percent of Muslims worldwide engage in kissing cousins. Due to male-female contact highly frowned upon, only cousins have access to each other. Guess what? Young people universally want to play, touch, grope, lick, suck, fuck - If allowed.

I tried to bone my female cousins; however, they would draw the line at penetration. You had to marry to get laid. Being a rising star, I was highly desired but was denied access to the restricted area of the kitty unless I was willing to tie the knot. I made out with many of my cousins, and I had dozens of them.

Cultural inbreeding has resulted in inferior mental capacity, lower IQ, and a host of other degenerative diseases. When you deal with most Pakistanis, you better prepare for a ride. They mean well but will boggle your mind with their bullshit - while looking at you with genuine sincerity. They don't even see that American drone policy is good for them that Americans are only targeting the sworn enemies of their own State.

If ordered by Allah, Muslims are willing to slaughter their own child. Who the hell are you? You are dog meat, pal. All Allah has to do is show up and whisper some bullshit in their ears while these madmen are snoozing. These are crazy motherfuckers. I am serious.

This episode speaks volumes about the mindset of practicing hardcore Muslims. There is an important distinction though. Most Muslims you and I come across, who claim to be Muslims, are not really true Muslims. They are hypocrites, who cherry pick routinely. I can count true practicing Muslims on a single hand.

When I say that I'm an Agnostic, at least I try and live my life as an Agnostic. An Agnostic acknowledges that he or she has no way of ascertaining if God exists. As an Agnostic I have no internal tussle, division or agony regarding my beliefs. Though I must admit it's a bit lonely, as my landscape is sparsely populated. I am devoid of jest, light-hearted banter and camaraderie with the masses. I couldn't care less, I would rather be alone than live a dishonest, confused and hypocritical life. I am in good company, at peace when I am alone.

I had to laugh at the following piece, which I thought I would share with you. If the fatwa has not been already issued on me by some crackpot, the lines below might seal the deal. I expect a cold shoulder from many pissed off friends, even family. A dear wannabe Muslim friend, while requesting anonymity emailed me this from Pakistan the other day. He is a General in the army. Read on;

There is no accounting for the logic of Muslims. Everyone seems to be wondering why Muslim terrorists are so quick to commit suicide. Let's take a look, shall we:

No Christmas

No television

No nude women

No burgers

No beer

Rags for clothes

Towels for hats

Constant wailing from some idiot in a tower 5 times a day

More than one wife

More than one mother-in-law

You can't shave

Your wife can't shave

Your wife is picked for you by someone else

And your wife smells worse than your donkey

Then they tell you that, when you die, it all gets better?

Well, no kidding...
It's not like it could get much worse.
THE MUSLIMS ARE NOT HAPPY!
They're not happy in Gaza
They're not happy in Egypt
They're not happy in Libya
They're not happy in Morocco
They're not happy in Iran
They're not happy in Iraq
They're not happy in Yemen
They're not happy in Afghanistan
They're certainly not happy in Pakistan
They couldn't be happy in Syria
They're not happy in Lebanon
SO, WHERE ARE THEY HAPPY?
They're happy in Australia
They're happy in Canada
They're happy in England
They're happy in France
They're happy in Italy
They're happy in Germany
They're happy in Sweden
They're happiest in the USA
They're happy in Norway
They're happy in Holland
They're happy in Denmark
Basically, they're happy in every country that is not Muslim.
And unhappy in every country that is!

WHO DO THEY BLAME?
Not Islam
Not their leadership
Not themselves
THEY BLAME THE COUNTRIES THEY ARE HAPPY IN!
AND THEN, they want to change those countries to be like...
THE COUNTRY THEY CAME FROM
WHERE THEY WERE UNHAPPY
Excuse me, but I can't help wondering...
How damn dumb can you get?
And there are a Billion of you.
Lord have mercy on this planet.
We are fucked!

EPILOGUE

A sexless life sucks. I don't know, how in the hell monks and priests can take a vow of celibacy. 'Well, just monks, (most priests are butt fucking the choir boys. Monks have to be boning each other!) It is one thing to lose your desire for sex, which I have, due to injury, but to be an able man or, to a lesser degree, a woman, and not want to screw is beyond me.

I recently learned that, beginning in 1906, Mahatma Gandhi vowed to abstain from sex. He was following the practice of 'Brahmacharia,' a Hindu spiritual path that attempts to eliminate desire. To test his self-restraint, (while his poor wife watched,) Gandhi habitually slept with two young, beautiful naked girls—one on each side—but refrained from having sex with these young women. He called it "a worthwhile experiment." In my heyday, if I had two naked young women lying next to me, I'd screw not one, but both of them and the Mahatama. Fuck Brahmacharia. Are you kidding me?

Decisions by the maker(s) of the universe ought to be accepted without too much fuss. Death doesn't have much meaning for me; it never did. I remember taking the news of my parents' deaths with similar stoicism and acceptance. I accept birth and death as the cycle of life over which we have no control—zero. Certainly we do have control over our reactions to it.

I have cultivated a philosophy of acceptance about matters over which we have no control, such as traffic jams, bad weather, spilled milk, crazy people, stupidity, and Assholes. We can either throw a fit—and most of us do—or we can shrug our shoulders, say *Fuck it*, and move on with life. People die, shit happens, prepare for such eventuality. People in Pakistan make death a huge deal. mourning for days, even weeks, with conspicuous wailing. The Shia sect of Islam mourns the death of Prophet Ali for months, and the Prophet was murdered centuries ago.

My unpretentious and smart daughter, Sheila, came for a visit from down under. She brought her boyfriend of few years, Jamal, a very delightful young man, an Aussie of Lebanese descent. I had taken a hard stand before their arrival. I had made up my mind that I would try everything in my power to oppose their relationship. I did not like the idea of her living, a planet away. I could not imagine seeing her only a couple of times a year and having my grandchildren, if any, not even get to know us. A girl needs her family, her support group, especially in challenging times.

I was going to demand that she returns to States. I wanted Sheila back with us. But a strange thing happened along the way. I met the couple, and observing them so happy, so natural and comfortable with each other made me take a pause. I thought of my own youth when I was in love (though more than once.) I had prepared a letter for him, accusing him of hijacking our daughter. It was a bitter letter with scathing allegations about her deserting us. I was going to ask him to return her to us.

I invited Jamal for a one-on-one lunch. I took him to our favorite Mediterranean cafe and ordered Australian wine that the cafe had. Minutes turned into eternity. My mind went through a metamorphosis. The slimy Caterpillar became a beautiful butterfly. I forgot about giving Jamal, the letter I had written with the poisoned pen. Sheila couldn't have made a better choice. I was so happy and proud of her. He was my man too.

I was totally won over by this rather dashing, cultured, a fascinating man. Jamal reminded me of my own youth: sly, shrewd, smart, hardworking and ambitious. He sensed and smartly addressed my concerns about the happiness and the future of my daughter. He focused like a laser beam on my grave concerns. This provocative Aussie was sweet, firm and convincing. Am I fooled? Time will tell.

I pity those who take him on, as he would be a formidable adversary. Sheila, who is already at par with the best of the best, will have to be vigilant and be on her toes to be an equal partner to this seemingly magnificent man. A no-nonsense executive wedded to his work, Jamal assured me that he is working toward a business model where Sheila can spend time with us. They could have homes in Los Angeles as well as in Australia, soon. I will see my daughter more often. He will take care of her; I need not worry. I instinctively trusted him.

This whiz-bang guy carries an air of confidence with a tinge of superiority, which would intimidate an ordinary person, not me. I liked that in him. I have been accused of the same all my life: Cocky, self-assured and holier than thou. Excessive self-confidence can be mistaken as being rude or cocky. I never have meant to give that impression, but I guess such assurance and confidence come from being good at what we do. Yes, some humility could be useful, and God knows, I try, but I can't help it, especially when I feel I'm surrounded by imbeciles. Winning by default?

To recap the lives of the characters in my exciting life;

Geena is still battling the temptations of her choice. Man, these temptations, once they find a home in your mind and body, they don't want to leave. She, despite rehab, threat of incarceration, still can't seem to shake off the drugs. She started to work with me as an apprentice, I was so excited. Business was coming alive, I was energized like never before. After few months, she drifted back to her lifestyle

Sheila continues to live her beautiful life in Australia. We stay in touch regularly. She has turned out to be my brightest star in the universe. It appears to us that Australia may have won her over. What wonder, a good man can do for you. We all deserve a loving partner, a soulmate, but at what cost??

My ex and I have an uneasy truce, which is holding presently, but slightest provocation could start the war. Her sis Naz and her daughter MK have moved from Texas to live with us. My darling, Naz and I have a deal, she has taken over my caregiving from my ex, who is now super busy with her boutique. MK is one of a kind, very special, different, a talented but starving artist. I love her. She is a tall, attractive, 30 years old virgin, looking for Mr. Right, who uniquely, must be brown - a fellow Muslim, good looking with a bright future, and a little tall. I say a very tall order.

My ex-girlfriend, Dar, devastated and heartbroken got scared of everything. Shooter (s) have her ID, which was in the purse. She moved away to Sacramento area to pursue her career at Davis University. Mutual friends tell me that she was in a shock for a long time, unable to love another. Years later finally she met a man, she could care for. I wish her well and thank her from the core of my heart, to have spent such quality time with me. I'll love that forever.

Ken still lives in Alaska, he broke up with his Japanese lover. Ken and Sam come visit me often. MM is still in prison. We write, stay in touch. Julia, the yogi, is married with two children. My business buddy SJ has retired to the wilderness of Alaska.

Mr. X and I are good friends. He might come back in my life and help me with past account of friendship. I am about to go visit him across the border in Rosarito beach. He says he has good plans for my future. I believe him. I have nothing to lose. Beware of a man who has nothing to lose.

Another ex-PAF friend, Hijazi, I used to party with decades ago, came to see me, after four decades. He was fasting hardcore. Hijazi told me that I was more like sixty-six years old, like Boli, Sam and Yaeger. Oh well, age 62 or 66, it really doesn't matter anymore. I personally feel very young. How young, I can't say, maybe 42… a boyish Smile!

Incredible me, as I write, I am not half the man I used to be, no pun intended. Going forward has lost its charm but I am determined to live a good life until the end. There is not that much life left in me. I used to watch sunsets regularly, religiously, no more. I have stopped working since April fools day 2014. Ex and I, who live together in separate rooms, on separate floors, we are not getting along. We try and avoid each other. Simmering hostilities. Many misgivings and mistrust.

I hate to share bad news, but I will, as it is heartbreaking and soul wrenching, but most of us would relate to it on a human level.

I have had a lovely lawyer friend, def, with whom I have had the pleasure of breaking the bread and drink bunch of red wines for last ten years plus. Being a connoisseur of wines, he taught me the art of mastering the wines. We used to hang out, light up the ganja and share the chalice - try to solve world's problems. He knew all my girls and had a huge crush on Sheila. He was married to Kitty, who had two young adult children. Def was madly in love with Kitty, who was his assistant for many years. Office romance turned serious, he divorced his previous wife and married his assistant, Kitty. My ex and I always doubted her sincerity and thought she was up to no good.

The relationship deteriorated to ugly level. Kitty called in the Police and got him arrested for physical abuse. Def is a sweet, soft soul, which I thought wouldn't hurt a fly. He took this dramatic breakup very adversely and wanted to commit suicide. We talked about how to end life, which is not as easy as you think. Three nights ago, Def texted me and asked me if I had a gun? Def texted that life for him is over. That the Bar and the courts are after him, that he wants to end it. WTF! I told him "No Def, I don't own a gun." and expected this to blow over. Well, my friends, you wouldn't believe this.

Two days later, I had a call from Ferry, his sister. A tearful message on my answering machine. She said that Def was dead that he killed himself. Gone, forever. Damn, just like that? I called her back and we talked, sobbed, cried, helpless! I wanted to kill that bitch, Kitty, who had just recently talked Def into installing a stripper's dancing pole in the middle of their living room, so she and her 22 year old could go up and down the pole. Def was so smitten, she could have the pole installed up his ass, he would see no problem with it, whatever Kitty wanted. Def, a handsome attorney in his late 40's, laughed "Dari, you are just jealous." It was beyond belief. I went to attend his celebration of life.

My options are limited. Having lived a full and joyous life, I have no regrets, no practical desires unmet. It has been an amazing ride, and I have no fear of death, retribution or the Judgment Day, Zero!

I tried to acquire a life in which I could be generous and cared so deeply about goodness that I felt compelled to share it, spread it. We have to find people we love and who love us back. We should never develop feelings that are not returned. We should develop skills to invest in the right people. We can't be at the center of the universe; I try to show up, listen, sing, dance and laugh.

I tried to be good to my friends and family, and strangers, without whom life would be barren, lonely and painful. School never ends, the classroom is everywhere and the exam comes at the very end.

I am living proof that, after acquiring life skills, one can take a plunge into this thing called, life. Experiment, explore and investigate what is best for you, on this smorgasbord of life choices. Even if you screw up, it's okay. You can redeem yourself and claim whatever it is that you strive for or deserve. You can party. You can get out of your 'Box' and take the risk, take a chance. Don't be afraid to fall. You can get up, dust off and move forward.

It was not that long ago when I admitted to myself that I was a cheat, a thief and a liar, a piece of shit. Look how proud a man, I have become. Shit happens!

My daughters must have acted as a mirror to reflect, and given me reasons to live a beautiful life for them. Letting them down was not an option. The end justified the means and the end is what I chose it to be. Everybody chooses what is right and what is wrong. Yes, I chose to be a bad boy once, but I made the correction, changed course and largely redeemed myself in my own, and my peers and family's eyes. It was not natural or easy, but the journey and the results were well worth the effort. fuck yeah!

I brought myself up to face a tectonic shift as I was inherently a bad boy. A toxic lava flowing that would kill everything in its path. People have a hard time accepting that the others may have changed, chiefly due to their own inability and capacity to change, adopt, and rise above the herd.

I pride myself as a loving father, a good man and a crook you can trust...wink.

What happened to me that night was an exception, an aberration. Things like that randomly and routinely happen to people; it was just my turn. I have no major wishes unmet. Wishes are useless anyway. Accept yourself at the core. You are who you are. No one or nothing can change you at this moment, only you can. Change comes with time and diligent effort, one baby step at a time.

This is a wonderful world. We can choose to live a good and honorable life. Yes, there is ugliness and rot, but we have the power to focus on the good and ignore the bad. Most people are good, the majority. Caligula is not scheming to screw your daughter. Not many of us wake up in the morning and resolve to spoil someone else's day, hurt someone or screw someone over. Stuff happens, accidents occur, people make mistakes. Let it go, learn to shrug our shoulders, say *Fuck it* and move on. Some People are so full of themselves, angry, bitter and unhappy. Eighty-six them. They will drag you down in their misery. Misery loves company.

Develop skills to recognize and spot the scowling assholes. You can't keep everyone happy, but you certainly can make 'you' happy. That could be the key. If it does come down to a serious conflict between you and another, then, of course, run over the fucking bitch or take the bastard down. If your livelihood, liberty, safety and pursuit of happiness are at stake, then do whatever it takes to level the field. Don't be a mouse. Cultivate a strong but loving image, a balanced life, eat well, embrace the challenge. You can, I have. Don't dig in the heels when wrong, verify, apologize, and move forward.

This is not a dress rehearsal. This is the only life we will get, a real life, let's stop the excessive worrying, whining, complaining, regretting and daydreaming. Let's make damn sure that our goals and our expectations are in line, consistent with our abilities and our resources.

Live a stress-free life to the fullest so that our memories will be part of our happiness. Be very gentle, kind, fair and judicious. Always look out for # one. Always, ALWAYS!

CPSIA information can be obtained at www.ICGtesting.com
Printed in the USA
LVOW04s1923010515

436906LV00014B/1167/P